I0221659

Granville O. Haller

# The Dismissal of Major Granville O. Haller, of the Regular Army, of the United States

by order of the secretary of war, in special orders, no. 331, of July 25th,

1863

Granville O. Haller

**The Dismissal of Major Granville O. Haller, of the Regular Army, of the United States**
*by order of the secretary of war, in special orders, no. 331, of July 25th, 1863*

ISBN/EAN: 9783337011444

Printed in Europe, USA, Canada, Australia, Japan

Cover: Foto ©ninafisch / pixelio.de

More available books at **www.hansebooks.com**

# THE DISMISSAL

OF

# MAJOR GRANVILLE O. HALLER,

OF THE

## REGULAR ARMY,

. OF

# THE UNITED STATES

BY ORDER OF THE

## SECRETARY OF WAR,

IN

SPECIAL ORDERS, No. 331, OF JULY 25th, 1863.

ALSO,

## A Brief Memoir of his Military Services,

AND

## A FEW OBSERVATIONS.

---

"They that have done the deed, are honorable :
"What private griefs they have, alas, I know not,
"That made them do 't ; they are wise and honorable,
"And will, no doubt, with reason answer you."
MARK ANTONY's Oration over CAESAR.

---

Paterson, N. J.
PRINTED AT THE DAILY GUARDIAN OFFICE,
BROADWAY, CORNER OF MAIN STREET.
1863.

# CORRECTIONS AND ADDITIONS.

On page 16th, line 26th, read : [Yet he picked up and brought away some Southern man's slave, and had his services when this letter was written. It was *the interference of Northern men with the slaves of Southern men* and not *slavery* itself that has proved "A CURSE" "*A year ago*," he says, "*I was a pro-slavery man, but I saw enough*"— During this year he was on shipboard, and the Planters were at war with the North, then, what could he have seen "*down south to change my views entirely ?*"]

On page 18th, line 23rd, insert 7 and 8, to read : "copied on pages 7 and 8."

Same page, line 27th, add to the words "and was strongly advised against it." This was in May last, two months after the charges had been sent to the War Department, and as the Secretary of War had not entertained them, it was considered a sufficient refutation, and on this ground the subject was dropped.

Next to last line, page 21st, read "this *averment.*"

Page 28th, line 22nd, read "*Nachitoches.*"

Page 39th the translator followed the French orthography of Father Pandosy, in Indian names. *Owvrai* is better known as *Owhi*, the brother-in-law of Kamiarken ; and *Sklon* as *Skilu-om*, a brother of this great chief.

Page 69th, line 24th, read : "to ascertain, if possible, the number approaching."

Pages 74 and 75, read : "defense of Wrightsville" and "defenses."

# THE DISMISSAL

OF

# MAJOR GRANVILLE O. HALLER,

OF THE

## REGULAR ARMY,

OF

## THE UNITED STATES.

————•————

WAR DEPARTMENT,  
ADJUTANT GENERAL'S OFFICE,  
WASHINGTON, D. C., July 25th, 1863.

SPECIAL ORDERS,  
No. 331.        [EXTRACT.]

By direction of the President, the following named officers are hereby dismissed the service of the United States :

Major Granville O. Haller, 7th U. S. Infantry, for disloyal conduct and the utterance of disloyal sentiments.

\*     \*     \*     \*     \*     \*     \*     \*     \*

By order of the Secretary of War,

    (Signed)      E. D. TOWNSEND,

Asst. Adj. General.

OFFICIAL :

    (Signed) ROBT. WILLIAMS, A. A. G.

DISCOVERY OF THE DISMISSAL, AND WHAT WAS DONE TO REPAIR THE
DAMAGES.

By the merest accident I heard of my dismissal, while on
duty, making out certain reports in York, Pa., and hastened to
Washington to learn the cause of it. On the 29th of July I
called at the War Department, and on inquiry I was informed
that one Clark H. Wells, a Lieut. Commander of the U. S.
Navy, had been recently there in person, calling the Secretary
of War's attention to a letter he had written some four months
before, and of which he (Wells) had furnished me a copy : that
this Naval Officer was thereupon sent before Colonel Joseph
Holt, the Judge Advocate General, U. S. Army, who examined
him and administered to him an oath, and then submitted a report with comments upon the statements.

The whole proceedings were done privately, without giving
me the slightest notice of any accusations being entertained
against me by the War Department, and, of course, I was de-
barred the privilege of meeting my accuser 'face to face and
of cross-examining him ; also, of proving by the direct testimony of an officer who was present, that the statements con-
tained in said Wells' letter to the Secretary of War were false.

I hastened back to York and there prepared a letter, some-
what in the form of a defence to serve me, in a measure, in place
of that regular defence which I had no opportunity before to
make. It was dated on the 8th of August, 1863, and will be
found in the concluding pages of this statement, in which I requested " the privilege of proving before a Court of Inquiry, or
properly authorized Court, that the report was made upon the
false testimony of an incompetent and irresponsible witness." 

Learning that the Honorable JEREMIAH S. BLACK, Ex-Attorney
General of the United States, under President Buchanan, intended shortly after to repair to Washington, and having found
him on all occasions a warm and consistent friend of mine, and
knowing moreover that Mr. STANTON was indebted to Judge
BLACK for the California cases which gave him prominence as
a Lawyer, and for suggesting him (Mr. STANTON) for Attorney-

General, while he (Judge BLACK) took charge of the Port-folio of the Secretary of State,—I requested Judge BLACK to do me the kindness to present my defence to the Secretary of War. This he has done, and was promised an answer, after careful perusal, yet the Secretary has not had the courtesy to reply as he promised. In the middle of September I again repaired to Washington, and there submitted the following applications, to wit :

EBBITT HOUSE,
WASHINGTON, D. C., September 15th, 1863.

*Hon. Edwin M. Stanton, Secretary of War ;*

SIR : I respectfully request that I may be furnished with a copy of the proceedings of Col. HOLT, Judge Advocate General, U. S. A., upon whose report I have been dismissed the service of the United States.

I am, Sir, very respectfully,
Your Obedient Servant,
GRANVILLE O. HALLER,
(late a Major 7th U. S. Infantry.)

This letter was returned to me with the following endorsement on the back, viz. :

"Respectfully returned to Major G. O. HALLER. The Secretary of War de-
"clines to accede to his request "
"By order of the Secretary of War.
(SIGNED)     JAS. A. HARDIE,
War Department, September 19th, '63.          A. A. G.
To G. O. HALLER, Esq., York, Pa."
(Received, York, September 23d, in the evening.)

The other application was as follows :

EBBITT HOUSE, WASHINGTON, D. C.
. September 16th, '63.

*Hon. Edw. M. Stanton, Secretary of War :*

SIR : I respectfully call your attention to my letter, dated at York, Penna., August 8th, 1863, and which was presented by the HON. JEREMIAH S. BLACK, Ex-Attorney General of the U. S., in which I asked for a *Court of Inquiry or properly authorized Court*, but have received no reply.

I beg leave to renew the subject, and respectfully request that I may be ordered or allowed to appear before the *Commission* now in session, in this city, which investigates cases where OFFICERS of the Army have been dismissed the service of the United States, without previously having had an opportunity of defending themselves from the charges alleged against them.

The special orders, No. 331. current series, announces that I have been dismissed for *"disloyal conduct and the utterance of disloyal sentiments,"* and Lieut.

Commander C. H. WELLS, U. S. Navy, has alleged against me as follows : *"Here's to a Northern Confederation and a Southern one while Lincoln is President.'* This was given in the shape of a toast to Major WHITING, and which called forth a severe rebuke from me, and which was the cause of my leaving him."

I wish to prove by the direct testimony of Major CHARLES J. WHITING, 2d U. S. Cavalry, that I *never* gave him such a toast, and that he did not leave me for this reason. And, by a cross-examination of the said Lieut. Commander WELLS, I wish to prove the real cause of his leaving me, and expose his unworthy conduct and character. I will prove that this same Lieut. Commander Wells, after having taken the new oath of allegiance, spoke of it to a visitor as having *"just performed the most painful act of his life, that he had been compelled to take the oath of allegiance or be dismissed from the service, and that his necessities had made him do this violence to his views regarding the war then commencing,"* or words of similar import. Also other items which will show how to estimate his statement.

I wish also to prove by the testimony of Brigadier General HAUPT, and Major General BURNSIDE that in December last, the time of his visit, my conduct was marked for its loyalty ; and by Major General COUCH, that at the time he (Wells) was in Washington personally endeavoring to create a doubt as to my loyalty, my conduct was truly loyal. I believe that I can prove by evidence that my conduct uniformly has been truly loyal. I have now in my possession the written testimony of Major Generals BURNSIDE and COUCH as to my loyalty. I trust that my actions will be better proof of my sentiments than mere words.

In my communication I have not asked to be reinstated. I have merely asked what I have been taught to regard in this country as a well established right—the right to face my accuser, to cross-examine him, and produce evidence which may rebut his accusations. I deem it a duty to my family, to my friends, and to my country, as well as to myself, to seek an investigation and prove that I have been misrepresented.

I beg leave to add that my circumstances require me soon to repair to Washington Territory, and I understand that Lieut Commander WELLS, U. S. Navy, will be sent to sea in a few weeks. I therefore respectfully request a speedy decision on my application.

I am, sir, very respectfully,
Your obedient servant,
GRANVILLE O. HALLER,
(Late Major 7th U. S. Infantry.

Not hearing from the War Department up to the morning of the 23d of September, I wrote the following letter :

YORK, PENNA, September 23d, 1863.

*My Dear Colonel:*

On handing you my two applications (one for a copy of Judge HOLT's proceedings in my case, and the other asking to be ordered before the Commission sitting in Washington to have my case investigated) you were kind enough to say that you would attend to them and give me an answer.

Allow me to ask : If you have forwarded any answer to those applications? If not, is there any reason why I should wait longer for an answer?

Had I been tried by a Court Martial you are aware that I would have been entitled to a copy of the proceedings in my case from the War Department. As the proceedings of Col. HOLT caused my dismissal it seems equally clear that I should be allowed a copy of the facts and of his comments.

I learned in Washington incidentally that the Commission (of which General RICKETTS is President, now setting in your city,) has investigated cases where officers had been dismissed for perhaps six months, and by this means established their innocence, and of cases where officers have been charged with forgery and other criminal acts. I am therefore aware of no serious objection to my case being referred to it.

If I can get no answer, or a refusal, the conclusion is forced upon me that the War Department would prefer that the public should believe that I have been guilty of "disloyal conduct," and have uttered "disloyal sentiments," and leaves me no other means of defence than to publish, as General Franklin has done, a pamphlet in vindication of my loyalty, and let the public judge between us.

I will esteem it a favor to receive from you a prompt reply, either officially or privately, to determine my future action.

I am, Dear Colonel, Truly Yours,

GRANVILLE O. HALLER.

Lieut. Col. JAS. A. HARDIE, Asst. Sec'y of War,
Washington, D. C.

This letter was delivered in the post office, and the same evening the endorsement on letter of September 15th came to hand. To this time, no other communication has been received, and I therefore submit the case as it is known.

THE CHARGES.

The following is a copy of the letter written to the Secretary of War, by *Clark H. Wells*, U. S. N., over four months before my dismissal, and the only charges known to me, as having been made.

NAVY YARD, }
PHILADELPHIA, March 3d, 1863. }

SIR : As a loyal officer of the U. S. Navy, it becomes my duty, however painful, to report to you, officially, Major GRANVILLE O. HALLER, U. S. A., now a Brevet Lieutenant Colonel Sixth Infantry, for uttering disloyal sentiments in my presence, on the night of December 16th or 17th, 1862, in his tent opposite

Fredericksburg, Va., such as these : "Here's to a Northern Confederation and a Southern one, while Lincoln is President." This was given in the shape of a toast to Major Whiting, and which called forth a severe rebuke from me, and which was the cause of my leaving him, and when I had declared my intention of doing so, in consequence of his disloyal language, he replied "that if his presence was so disagreeable to me, he would procure as a companion to share with me his tent, a Black Republican, and he would go elsewhere." He had also said on a former occasion, "that he considered the President responsible for the loss of life at the battle of Fredericksburg." I enclose to you copies of two letters addressed to Major now Brevet Lieut. Col. HALLER, and extract from his in relation to this matter, which I conceive to be my duty to lay before you.

I will furnish a copy of this letter to Major, now Brevet Lieutenant Colonel Haller.

Respectfully yours,<br>
C. H. WELLS,<br>
Lieut. Commander, U. S. ·N.

Hon. E. M. STANTON, Secretary of War, Washington City, D. C.

DIRECT TESTIMONY.

The Major Whiting, alluded to as the officer to whom I gave a toast, is MAJOR CHARLES J. WHITING, 2ND U. S. CAVALRY, who, on my sending him recently·a copy of Wells' letter, writes :

PORTLAND, ME., September 27th, 1863.

*My Dear Major:*

Yours of the 23d I received yesterday, also a copy of C. H. WELLS' letter to the Secretary of War. I say without any hesitation, that upon the time referred to in his letter, you never proposed such a toast, as he says you did, or uttered any sentiments which a *true* lover of his country might not have uttered, even as an officer of the army. I cannot recollect the whole conversation ; but my recollection of the general tenor of it is very distinct—and I think Lieut. WELLS first got offended with you, upon your asking him why he had not crossed the pontoon bridge ? which question was drawn from you by WELLS' insinuating, that you had always remained at Headquarters. You are at liberty to show this letter to any of your friends, and state publicly or in print, that I pronounce Lieut. WELLS' statement in regard to you, in connection with my name, as false in spirit, as well as letter.

Yours truly,<br>
CHAS. J. WHITING.

Received at York, Pa., October 3d, 1863, on my return from Chambersburg, Pa.

But the accusations date back to December 16th or 17th, 1862, at which time MAJOR GENERAL BURNSIDE was in command. Desirous of knowing, whether or not he was satisfied with my conduct and loyalty, after I had been accused of "disloyal senments" by this unfortunate Wells, I addresed a note to him, and received the following reply :

HEADQUARTERS DEPARTMENT OF THE OHIO, }
CINCINNATI, O., March 27, 1863. }

*Major Granville O. Haller, Headquarters Army Potomac:*

MY DEAR MAJOR : I take great pleasure in answering yours of the 22d inst., and awarding to you my cordial approbation of your services while under my command.

The interest, skill, and loyalty you have always manifested in the performance of your duties, was a subject of comment at our Headquarters, and the result of your labors was always satisfactory.

Your faithful services, both before the breaking out of this rebellion, and since the commencement of the war, have given abundant proof to the public of your devotion to your country, and your friends who have known you need no evidence to substantiate your loyalty and true patriotism.

I regret that you find it necessary to ask to be relieved from your post, and trust your health may soon allow you to return to duty in the field.

I am, Sir,

Very truly yours,

A. E. BURNSIDE, Maj. Gen.

At the time this unfortunate Wells was in Washington, personally playing the part of an *Informer*, I was employed by MAJOR GENERAL COUCH, as an Extra Aide-de-camp, and busily engaged, at remote points from him, in organizing the militia ; obstructing the roads in the South Mountain ; directing military operations ; and with a few score of mounted men, observing the enemy, and keeping the General advised of the Rebel movements, in Adams and York Counties.

In a private letter I had the honor to receive from GENERAL COUCH, after he had learned the alleged grounds for my dismissal, alluding to the cause of it, he writes that it "perfectly astounded me, never dreaming but that you were as loyal as myself."

On the 27th of June, 1863, alluding to my services in the neighborhood of Gettysburg, in a telegram to me he says: " Your assistance has been invaluable."

And, in an " official" letter, he writes as follows:

HEAD QUARTERS, DEPARTMENT OF SUSQUEHANNA,
Chambersburg, August 13, '63.

*Major G. O. Haller, York, Pa.:*

DEAR SIR : I duly received your letter of the 28th inst., transmitting reports of your operations at Gettysburg, York, Columbia, &c., while serving in the capacity of Aide-de-camp on my Staff.

Having carefully read these reports, I was impressed with the energy, action and good judgment displayed by you at the time of the invasion. Without any organized force at the commencement of it, you, with the aid of loyal citizens of Gettysburg and vicinity, were enabled to make a show of resistance to the invaders, and keep this department, and therefore the General Government, well informed of rebel movements.

Your services were valuable to the country. For this Department I express to you my thanks.

You can leave to your children the proud heritage that when your State was threatened by the fearful calamity of rebel invasion you were among the very foremost of its defenders.

I am very respectfully,

Your Obedient Servant,

D. N. COUCH,

Major General.

Here I might allow my case to rest. The testimony of *Major Whiting* and of *Major Generals Burnside and Couch* are consistent and conclusive. Although actions are better evidence than words, the words themselves are here conclusive.

But this is not the only testimony I have to produce. I will show before closing my defence that this unfortunate Wells has been a Democrat, a Secessionist, and a Republican and Negro Sympathizer, which are not only inconsistent but cannot fail to excite a lively mistrust in his love for truth and for fixed principles. But at the date, the 16th or 17th of December, he was stopping with me as *my guest*, yet he ignores the rules of hospitality, and endeavors to injure me, for he tells Mr. Stanton of a toast I should have given Major WHITING, which caused him to give me a severe rebuke, then leave my tent, never to come near it again so far as his letter goes. His language in this letter plainly tells that he could not any longer hold intercourse with me—one so disloyal as myself. But I will now present a few of his letters to me after this event, *to give the lie from his own lips to this idea*, thrown out by him to gull Secretary STANTON. He says that I gave that toast, on the 16th or 17th of December. Now only two or three days after this, he wrote to me as follows:

YORK, PA., December 19, 1862.

*My Dear Major:*

I arrived home safely in a few hours after leaving General Franklin's tent, and found all the folks well. Mrs. Haller and the children took supper with us last evening, and had you been present you would have enjoyed the oysters, which were very fine indeed. I enjoyed them the more, as my appetite had been sharpened by my *brief* campaign in Virginia.

I gave your wife all the news, and when I had done, I found that I had not imparted anything that she had not seen in the papers. The people, as well as I can judge, are not dispirited in the least; those who sympathize with the South are exultant as a matter of course, and would no doubt give expression to their thoughts if they thought they could do so with impunity. [Here he admits that he has not heard of a single instance where a person has given expression to his thoughts, but it *is a matter of course*, in his mind, that there are Southern sympathizers and that they are exultant. Is not a clause like this mere slander?]

All admire the gallant conduct of Franklin, inasmuch, that his friends here are going to present him with a sword, which he is certainly deserving of, and which he will no doubt appreciate. [On my return to York, I found that the statement about the presentation of a sword was a mere freak of his imagination!]

There is nothing else going on in town; even the battle of Saturday last is little talked of, which shows the phlegmatic character of our population.

I travelled to Washington in company with Lieut. B., (Corps of Engineers), and learned from him that you had had another entertainment, the effects of which he felt in the shape of a headache. How did you stand it? I am afraid that these little social gatherings tend to make you express yourself too openly on political subjects, which some civilian might take advantage of, and use it to your prejudice, and so I would caution you to be more guarded. [Does not this imply *that he would scorn*, as all officers would, to take advantage of, and use to my prejudice, any opinions I express in the privacy of my tent to friends?]

I shall ever recollect my visit to the Army, and bear witness to the bravery and devotion of our troops. It has made a most pleasant impression upon my mind, and I am more confident than ever of our ultimate success.

Remember me kindly to Captain Cushing and to Major Whiting; also those whose names I cannot now recollect.

Lieut. Spaulding, 2d Cavalry, was kind enough to loan me his horse, when I rode to Franklin's Headquarters. I returned him the next day by an Orderly from Franklin's Corps. I hope he arrived safely, as he had been well taken care of.

Thank Mr. Spaulding for me for his horse and kind attentions ; also Dr. Wilson, who lives in the same tent with him.

I saw the Asst. Secretary of the Navy for a moment, and he assured me that I should be ordered as Captain of the Philadelphia Navy Yard ; so I shall soon leave.

If I can be of any service to you let me know. I saw your brother this morning, and gave him a brief account of yourself, and the military operations before Fredericksburg.

Look out for the bridge over the Potomac Creek, I came across in an open car, and, I felt very much like a man suspended by a wire. Let me hear from you soon.

Sincerely yours,<br>C. H. WELLS, U. S. N.

Here he says : "IF I CAN BE OF ANY SERVICE TO YOU LET ME KNOW." Is this the language to be expected from him, after writing such statements to Mr. STANTON ? In this letter he makes a direct allusion to my political opinions, but shows most clearly that he was not offended at them, and would scorn to take advantage of them or use them to my prejudice, but it occurred to him that *some civilian* might, and he therefore cautioned me to be more guarded. But so innocent was I of having said anything on political subjects which could possibly injure me with an honorable man, that, in my reply, I wrote him that all I had said I would not hesitate to repeat, even before the President, if he desired to learn my views. This letter from him, standing by itself, will satisfy the most skeptical that my political opinions had not offended the unfortunate man, nor caused him to leave my tent.

But sometime about midnight, perhaps one o'clock in the morning, he left my tent " in a huff" to sleep elsewhere, and he labors hard to connect it with the imaginary toast that I gave to Major WHITING. As Major WHITING unhesitatingly declares that I never gave any such toast, it is evident that he labors under some hallucination, or is lending himself to some "hell-born" scheme—borrowing one of his favorite adjectives. And here, perhaps, it will be proper to show the real cause of this "much ado about nothing."

On the evening in question, I had unexpectedly received some Scotch whisky, and as some friends came in I offered them a hot punch, and, of course, gave, to *my guest* at the same time. He drank cautiously, but as officers came in, at different times, he drank often, and by midnight, the punch, I have supposed, had affected his mind so far as to show peculiarities of his disposition. I had taken the pains to explain to him the difficulties, the causes of delay, and failure of the Peninsular Campaign. I spoke of South Mountain and Antietam as proofs of Gen. McClellan's abilities, and I expressed regret that at the moment the General was leading his successful Army through Virginia, and had expressed his expectation in four or five days more to be in a position to compel the enemy to fight him on a field of his own choosing, and we knew the Army of the Potomac never before was in better fighting condition, and therefore we all felt confident of great results.—I explained to him that it was not necessary to attack the Confederate Army behind intrenchments at Culpepper C. H., if we could reach the Railroad from Richmond without it : the supplies from Richmond once cut off, the intrenchments would be of little value : and the Army of the Potomac once between Lee's Army and Richmond would have great advantages in its favor—but the election in New York having turned against the Administration, it was followed by the removal of General McClellan, and all our prospects on his proposed line of march were given up ; for the new commander adopted a different line and plan of operations. Thus, for the victories we anticipated, we had now to mourn over the disasters at Fredericksburg. I thought the interference of the Administration had changed certain victory into disaster. I deprecated politics when it was allowed to interfere with the management of Armies : that the interference had brought about heavy losses and defeat at Fredericksburg, and the Administration were in this light responsible for the losses and all the consequences which should follow from the change. But Mr. Wells saw that this view would not inspire the people with confidence

in what he called "the government" and intimated that I ought
to take some other view, "for it is the duty of all officers to
sustain the Government." I then explained to him the difference between "the Government" and "the Administration."
That when the Administration was controlled by the Constitution and the Laws of Congress, and its actions regulated by pure
Patriotism, then I believed every officer and the whole country
should and would support it. But I left it to him to say if the removal of McClellan was *from Patriotic or from Party motives?*
And his reply was that he thought I was a "little" disloyal. I
then reminded him of my conduct at Fredericksburg, to let my
actions speak for my loyalty. He stood by, when Brig. Gen.
Haupt, Railroad Engineer, had told me that two hundred soldiers and his carpenters, while the firing was going on at Fredericksburg, had abandoned their work at the R. R. Bridge, and
he could not get on with the work. I then volunteered to furnish him with one hundred men of General Headquarters' Guard
—the 93d N. Y. Vols.—if General Burnside would approve of it
and I would remain with them and guarantee that none would
quit, nor allow his workmen to quit, merely for the firing. Yet,
to this service, I received for answer "*that there was no danger
in it.*" Now, as he and I had been that day in Fredericksburg,
and each was careful to cross the pontoon bridge during the in-
tervals between the enemy's cannonading, I asked him "Why
he had not crossed the pontoon bridge when I did?" He instantly flared up and asked "Do you mean to say that I was
afraid?" as if I had imputed an unmanly fear to his action, and
from this time he manifested a determination to leave me. He
asked Major Whiting if he might sleep in his tent, intimating
that I was disloyal, although he had never before met Major
Whiting, who was at a loss to understand his conduct. I then
offered him my tent to himself, saying he could take my bed
and I would sleep in some friend's tent: but he answered that
he would not turn me out of my tent. I then offered "to get
him a tent to sleep in, with some Black Republican." But instead of appreciating my offer, he insisted upon sleeping in Major Whiting's tent, without being invited, and packed up his car-

pet bag to accompany him. Upon my requesting Major WHI-
TING to take him along, he kindly consented to do so.

Poor fellow! I believed then that the punch he had taken
had affected his brain, and I dreaded the consequence, for it
might bring back a serious attack of his old infirmity, which
had placed him under the charge of the physicians in the Pennsylvania Hospital for the Insane at Philadelphia, for some three
months, the year previous. I saw that he was wild, if not beside himself, but I did not dream that he labored under hallucinations, and could forget the conversation of that night. The
next afternoon, the excitement had passed off, and he came voluntarily to my tent, when I told him that I had feared that his
old infirmity had returned; but he begged me not to say anything about the previous evening, and there the matter dropped,
he going off to York, Pa., a very cordial friend. It was quite a
surprise to me to hear him, a month afterwards, give his recol-
lections of that night in the extraordinary manner in which he
presents it. He writes:

NAVY YARD, PHILADELPHIA, }
January 16, 1863. }

*Major Haller:*

MY DEAR SIR: I should have replied to your letter before, but ever since my
arrival at this station I have been kept very busy, and when night comes, I feel
too tired to do anything but smoke and chat with the children; after all there is
nothing like one's home, which you have doubtless experienced for so many
years.

Mrs. ——— is here on a visit for the purpose of procuring some little com-
forts for her brother, whom we saw. I am pleasantly situated, having for the
first time in my naval career, a Government house to live in, but which I was
obliged to furnish to some extent. Were it not that I have been away a year in
the S. A. Squadron and for the sake of my family, I would prefer going to Sea in
these exciting times, although my naval friends tell me that I have done my
share; I think not, for I believe that no officer can do too much to assist in crushing out this sinful rebellion.

During my short visit to Gen. Franklin with whom I have been intimate for
many years, I was glad to see that he was thoroughly Union in his sentiments,
and had a horror of anything like disloyalty or secession. I have ever entertained a high opinion of his abilities as a man and as a soldier. The sword
which will be presented to him will have inscribed upon it all the battles he has
been engaged in. [This was a most deliberate falsehood, for there was no sword.]

I heard from others in the camp that his bravery in the battle of Fredericksburg was of the highest order, and that alone entitles him to the distinguished honor of having a sword given him.

You mention in your letter that anything you may have said concerning the manner in which this war was carried on you would not hesitate to repeat. [So far as my statements went, I would not hesitate to repeat *them*, but what he here says I uttered, the reader will see by Maj. WHITING's letter, "*is false in spirit as well as in letter*."] At least I judge so. Do you recollect proposing the toast to Maj. WHITING? and which was the occasion of my leaving your tent. "*Here's to a Southern Confederacy, and a Northern one during the Administration of Lincoln,*" and another expression you had made use of before, in charging the President with loss of life in the battle of Fredericksburg, and that you believed "that it was the intention of the Administration to sacrifice the Army of the Potomac in the neighborhood of Richmond. [This charge he voluntarily abandons in his letter to Secretary STANTON.] If these are your sentiments I would not hesitate to proclaim them, and were I to entertain such, I should resign my Commission. I do not mention these matters with a view of renewing any or causing unpleasant feeling, but merely to show you that you are doing yourself an injustice, *for I cannot believe that you think so,* [Here he admits the above are not my sentiments!] otherwise you would not remain in the Army. Were the opinions you have expressed before me and others made known, it would be exceedingly prejudicial to you. In these times it is the duty of all officers to sustain the Administration in the suppression of this rebellion. No mid-way course can be taken.

A year ago I was, what is termed a pro-slavery man, but I saw enough while down South to change my views entirely, for I regard Slavery as a curse to our Country, and the cause of this hell-born rebellion. [Yet he ██████ and brought away a negro and has his services now!]

I believe there is nothing new in York ; I have no affection for that place, as it contains a strong disloyal element, chiefly confined to those who have not shouldered the musket. If you should visit the city, I hope you will let me know. I regret very much to hear of the accident to Capt CUSHING but I hope ere this he has entirely recovered. This horseback riding I have always considered dangerous, I therefore never mounted a horse without feeling uncomfortable. Nothing like a ship after all.

That Galveston affair we all deplore, being the only mishap to our Navy since the breaking out of the rebellion. We lost four good officers by the premature blowing up of one of the Steamers. The "Petapsco," a new Monitor was here two weeks ago. I regard her as invulnerable. She carries a gun weighing forty-one thousand pounds, and throws a ball of 450 lbs. service, charge of powder 35 lbs., also a two-hundred pound rifle. Altogether she is a most formidable vessel.

Kind regards to Maj. WHITING. Did Lieut. Spaulding of his regiment receive the horse which I had returned by one of Gen. FRANKLIN's orderlies? Kind regards to Capt. GIBSON and FRANKLIN, should you meet with them. Let me hear from you, and believe me to be

Yours sincerely,

C. H. WELLS, U. S. N.

As Major WHITING was a disinterested witness, who had seen all and heard all that was said, I desired him to write a letter to Wells on purpose to remove the hallucination under which he seemed to labor. But the Major was in Washington on Court martial duty, and that duty generally being temporary, I expected him back almost daily, but before he returned, I received the following letter :

NAVY YARD,<br>
PHILADELPHIA, February 17th, 1863.

*Major Haller :*

MY DEAR SIR : Since I wrote you in reply to your letter, I have thought so much over what had occurred in your tent, and which was the cause of my leaving you, that I cannot see why I should not report your disloyal language to the Secretary of War, painful as it may be. [This expression is undoubtedly used to prepare my mind for the closing passage. "No one can doubt my loyalty, and I hope you will give me the credit of performing my duty conscientiously." Now it has come to my knowledge, and I can show by two witnesses, that this unfortunate man has spoken of an officer of the U. S. Navy, high in rank, as having a son who was at sea with the South Atlantic Squadron, and this son was in correspondence with the Rebels and was helping them, or words of similar import ; and when he was asked why he had not reported the case to the Navy Department, the reply was : "It would only do me harm—it would bring down the Commodore on me," or words to this effect ; showing how "*conscientiously*" he has been performing his duty!] but in these times when we are engaged in a deadly struggle to sustain our Government, I would sacrifice my son.

You uttered this expression in my presence, "Here's to a Northern Confederation and to a Southern one, while Lincoln is President," which you gave as a toast to Major Whiting in your tent, and had also said "that you considered the President responsible for the loss of life at the battle of Fredericksburg." No one can doubt my loyalty, and, I hope you will give me the credit of performing my duty conscientiously.

I am yours,<br>
C. H. WELLS,<br>
Lieut. Commander, U. S. N.

Immediately on the receipt of the above letter, I wrote to him, as follows :

YORK, PENNA., February 18th, 1863.

*Lieut. Commander Clark H. Wells, U. S. N., Commanding Navy Yard, Phila :*

MY DEAR SIR : Your letters of the 16th of January and 17th of February, are received, and contents noticed.

2

The absence of Major WHITING, U. S, A., on a Court Martial at the city of Washington, prevented my laying before him the former of the two letters, and getting from him a denial of the statements which you make, and then replying to yours. I shall not ask you to take my own statements. Fortunately, there was a witness present on the occasion of the conversation referred to in your letters, *who saw all, heard all,* and *knows all* that occurred.

I have not seen him since the receipt of your letters, and I think when called upon, he will remove the hallucination under which you seem to labor.

One thing I remember, and can hardly think that you have forgotten it. I gave *a toast, and only one,* it was :

      "THE CONSTITUTION AS IT IS : THE UNION AS IT WAS!"

If this is *disloyalty,* then as Patrick Henry says : "Make the most of it!"

In the frame of mind in which you have written, it is obvious that all previous relations, however agreeable, are ignored. I shall not trouble you, therefore, with an account of your friends, or the *on dits* of this place.

As a Mason it is my duty to respect you as a brother, but I trust you will so conduct your course towards all brethren, that *discord* may not be charged upon you.

Fraternally yours,

G. O. HALLER.

He became impatient however, and on the 4th of March he forwarded to me a copy of his letter to the Secretary of War, of March 3d, 1863, copied on page —. As soon as my duties permitted, I wrote to him the subjoined letter, which discharged the matter from my mind, until dismissed, excepting once, when in York, I proposed to some masonic friends to have this matter investigated, and was strongly advised against it.

CAMP NEAR FALMOUTH, VA.,
March 20th, 1863.

*C. H. Wells, Lieut. Commander, U. S. N. :*

MY DEAR SIR : Your letter of March 4th, enclosing a copy of your letter to the Hon. E. M. STANTON, Secretary of War, reporting me "for uttering disloyal sentiments in my [your] presence" is received. I have now waited over two weeks to learn what course the War Department would pursue on your statements—perhaps you can tell. They have not even asked for an application.

It is due to myself to say, that in passing through Washington, on the 24th of February, I called on Major WHITING and showed him your letters, and a copy of mine to you of February 19th, in which I promised or assumed that he would make a statement which I had promised to forward to you. He then offered to write one, and as I would leave next morning too early to get it, he was to forward it to me here. He returned on the 5th inst., and on the 6th called at my tent and stated that he had forgotten to write. Having stated to you masonically that I thought when he was called upon, ho would give you a statement which would remove the hallucination under which you seem to labor. I was entitled as a Mason to a hearing ; but your haste indicates rather an over-zealous desire to open a correspondence with the Honorable Secretary of War, than conform to obligations and preserve your honor and character from a foul blot. I take it for granted that the Secretary of War will refer your letter to Major WHITING, and I trust will allow me to bo heard in the case. I feel safer in his hands than, I am sorry to say, I would in yours, and the day will come, I trust, when I can have this matter investigated by the Masonic Lodge in York, and your conduct sifted and stamped as it deserves.

In your letter of Feb. 20th, you write, "I shall not dwell upon personal allusions as the matter has, in my opinion, taken an official character." This may be your opinion, but the society in which I have been schooled for the last twenty-three years does not allow an officer or gentleman to accept the hospitalities of another as a friend and then go off and comment on what he has seen or heard to that friend's prejudice : much less can he cover himself with his official character when he is not there in his official capacity. But aside from the violations of hospitality and courtesy, there is a question of veracity in your statements.

I have heretofore abstained from commenting on your conduct and your lectures to me, in your letters, from motives of delicacy. I had no wish to lend myself in any way to produce an open rupturo of our social relations. You must do me the justice to admit in your heart, that you have thrust this issue upon me. You have repeatedly thrust at me your charges of disloyalty, after I told you that I would not ask you to take my own statements, but agreed to leave it to one who saw all, heard all, and knew all that took place. You will yet learn that your statement to the Honorable Secretary of War is false.

It is now my turn to lecture you a little and hold up to your gaze a few reflections of your own, for I hold that the old truism "*Actions speak louder than words*," is a self-evident fact, and by this test I am prepared to compare our *Patriotism*.

You saw me in Fredericksburg hasten to the wounded man and aiding there. You know that I volunteered, (when my duties excused me from service which might expose my person to danger,) to furnish one hundred men of my command and stay with them to fix the R. R. Bridge, because two hundred men had that day fled from that duty. ·You know too that I am in the field and that Generals BURNSIDE and HOOKER have retained me in my old position under Gen. McCLELLAN, and they at least are satisfied with my loyalty and the discharge of my duties.

How is it with you? Your patriotism stands mostly on paper. In your letter of January 16th you write : "*that I* [you] *had been away a year.*" [Now think of it, you were "*away a year !*" Why, thousands of volunteers left their homes, with business unsettled, and have been away *two years !*] *and for the sake of my* [your] *family* [think, too, you have said you are ready "to sacrifice your son," yet *your family* prevents you doing your duty, for you say] *I* [you] *would prefer going to sea in these exciting times, although my naval friends tell me that I have done my share.* I THINK NOT, *for I believe that no officer can do too much to assist in crushing out this sinful rebellion."* Here then, *family considerations* are acknowledged to have *crushed out* your patriotism, for you think that *you have not* done your share —that you cannot do too much. While you here admit that loyalty and patriotism require your services at sea, yet you have sought at the Navy Department for the order placing you in a peaceful station. This is your boasted loyalty, and in your letter of February 17, you say: *"no one can doubt my* [your] *loyalty."* I have found, by experience, that the most sanctimonious members of a church— those who intrude their religious feelings on all around them—are the most hypocritical, and have motives for displaying their outward piety. The truly pious man retires to the inner closet and there offers up his devotions. He lets his conduct speak of his moral qualities. So in all relations, I look at a man's actions, not at his professions and boastings, and make up my mind. In your letter of February 17, written from the quiet Navy Yard at Philadelphia, your patriotism reaches the climax. You say : *" When* WE *are engaged in a deadly struggle to sustain* [I suppose you *unintentionally* omitted the words *"the constitution of"*] *our government, I would sacrifice my son."* Had this passage been prepared at sea, while devoting your life as a sacrifice, if necessary, to your bleeding country, it might pass for noble patriotism, [although repugnant to our animal instincts, and evincing a most unnatural frame of mind,] but, while you take such good care of your own life, it sounds very much like *buncombe!*

Before that GOD, whom you profess to worship—who knows our hearts—and who understands our motives—I can fearlessly submit my loyalty and yours, and ask him to judge between us.

There are several passages in your letters, which might be noticed in addition to those above. But enough of this. I trust that I may be able soon to get to York, and there I can get an investigation which will decide how far your charges of disloyalty go, and disinterested brethren judge between us.

Very respectfully, your obedient servant,

G. O. HALLER,
Major 7th Infantry.

### THE APPLICATION FOR A COURT OF INQUIRY.

The following is the letter first submitted to the Secretary of War, and the Reader will perceive, after perusing the evidence before him of my loyalty, and of my arduous services, that my case is presented in a calm and argumentative manner, designed to impress the Secretary of War with its truthfulness, then ask as a matter of sheer justice to myself, for an official investigation, believing that it is a right, which cannot be questioned, that an Officer should have a thorough investigation into any charges, if he declares them to be untrue. An Officer's character and honor are more to him than his life, or wealth, and if they can be arbitrarily taken from him, as in my case, the Officers of the Army must soon, indeed, become mere instruments of the Secretary to enforce his will, whether in support of Law or not. The application is as follows :

York, Pa., August 8th, 1863.

*Hon. Edwin M. Stanton, Secretary of War.*

Sir : On the 29th ult., I received a copy of Special Orders No. 331, which informed me that, " by direction of the President" I was " dismissed the service of the United States for disloyal conduct and the utterance of disloyal sentiments."

By this order I am deprived of the profession for which my education and life long habits have fitted me, and I am driven from it, covered with whatever of infamy the recorded condemnation of the highest authority can bring on my character. The statements which brought this about, *being untrue*, I hope it is not too late to get justice. At all events, I take the liberty to give you *a true statement* of my case, which, perhaps, may serve me in place of that regular defence which I have had no opportunity to make. Some vindication of myself I certainly owe to my family and my friends.

Undoubtedly an order which may consign an officer to ruin and disgrace, ought to be placed on specific and intelligible grounds. "Disloyal conduct" and "disloyal sentiments" are phrases unknown to any law civil or military, and have come into fashion of late, as mere party catchwords, signifying anything or nothing, according to the notions of the persons who use them.

That I am or have ever been really disloyal in word, thought, or deed, is utterly and nakedly false. From the time I first entered the army, nearly twenty-four years ago, I have been true and faithful to my country, her government, her constitution and her laws. And this avertment never has been, and never will be controverted by the testimony of any man who is *honest* and *sane*. My services vouch for this. I was in much of the *Florida war* : through all the *Mexican war*, and in most of the battles from PALO ALTO to EL MOLINO DEL REY and CAPTURE OF THE CITY OF MEXICO inclusive. • I was engaged in several Indian Wars on the Pacific Coast and elsewhere, and in this Rebellion from its commencement until notified of my dismissal. I have never failed in the performance of any duty however difficult or dangerous, and I have never been charged with a single act of insubordination. I think I can say without boasting that I have enjoyed far beyond many officers the friendship of my associates and the approbation of my superiors in the service. The official reports on file in your Department, and printed in the Congressional Documents, will not only show this, but will prove that my behavior in every important battle, won from the Commanding Officers, expressions of the highest praise. I speak with the pride which becomes a soldier, when I say that my record is without stain.

Almost contemporaneously with the base accusations of Wells, MAJOR GENERAL BURNSIDE was writing the warmest eulogium on my fidelity to the cause of the Union : and only a few days before my dismissal, MAJOR GENERAL COUCH gave me the strongest evidence of his confidence, and of the high appreciation in which he held what he was pleased to call " *the invaluable assistance*" I had rendered him, in retarding the advance of the enemy in their march towards Philadelphia.

I am not now, I have never been, and it is likely I never will be a Politican. That is not my trade ! I have interfered in no canvass, have written nothing for newspapers, and spoken at no public meetings. But I have held opinions on Public Affairs which, as they do not change when the civil administration changes, are sometimes favorable and sometimes unfavorable to the party in power. To these opinions, I have occasionally, in the freedom of private conversation, given moderate, fair, and inoffensive expression. This non-intervention in the political disputes of the people is the custom of service among the best officers of the Regular Army, and I have followed it because it has the approbation of my judgment and my conscience : and this freedom of opinion has been conceded to officers of the Army from the foundation of this Republic, and never has been questioned until now.

One *Clark H. Wells*, a Lieutenant Commander in the U. S. Navy, had a conversation with Major CHARLES J. WHITING, 2nd U. S. Cavalry, and myself, on or about the 17th December, 1862, (over seven months ago,) at my tent, on the Rappahannock, in which politics were mentioned, and it is upon his false and perverted statements of that private conversation that my dismissal is grounded. Those statements were referred to some subordinate in your office, and upon those alone I was found guilty of disloyalty, reported for dismissal, and actually dismissed. I now appeal to your sense of justice and ask you whether that is the fair play to which an officer of twenty four years' service, with an unblemished record, is entitled? Who, in the army is safe, if the War Department opens its ear to the base whispers of every paltry spy, who treacherously takes advantage of an officer's hospitality and becomes an informer to curry favor with the dispensers of patronage? Apart from the individual wrong which such a practice must produce, can anything be better calculated to demoralize the Army and bring the service, as well as the Government itself, into disrepute?

Conversations are proverbially unreliable as evidence. They are so easily misunderstood, and so difficult to remember that there is not one instance in many thousands where the casual talk of a man can be reproduced with accuracy even by respectable witnesses. Nay, where is the man who can repeat exactly what he himself has said but yesterday? If conversations are of small account when detailed with all possible fairness, they become contemptible when tattled by a man of weak understanding and malicious heart.

I here aver that I never uttered the words imputed to me by Wells, nor any words of similar import, either at the time he refers to, or at any other time in my life. He says I drank to a Southern Confederacy during this Administration. This is merely and simply false. I can prove my denial to be true by the direct testimony of MAJOR WHITING, (before mentioned,) a gentleman whose honor and veracity no one who knows him will doubt. The only toast given by me on that occasion was this: "Here's to the Constitution as it is, and the Union as it was!" which I thought then and think now, expresses a sentiment perfectly patriotic and most purely loyal.

Why did MR. WELLS make this false statement ? Let me tell you. *The man is crazy.* Yes : the witness upon whose *ex-parte* statements your department has endeavored to bring ruin to me and my family *is a lunatic !* It was only on the 11th of October, 1861, that he was released from the Pennsylvania Hospital for the Insane at Philadelphia, and the act was accompanied by the written regret of the Medical Officer in charge, at seeing him leave before he was entirely well. I have known him for a long time ; on my return to Camp, near Falmouth, Va., from York, Pa., he asked to accompany me to see an intimate friend. Thinking him harmless, I did not refuse : on the contrary, shared with him my tent and table, until he found his friend. He was there not merely as *my* guest, but a self-invited guest, and under the greater obligations to respect the hospitality.

On the occasion to which his statements refer, he drank some punch, not excessively but enough to inflame his weak brain and aggravate his mental disease, which gradually irritated his morbid temper, and fixed his malice upon myself. He imagined that I had insinuated an unmanly fear on his part in crossing the Rappahannock river, during the firing of the enemy. He asked MAJOR WHITING, whom he had met for the first time, to let him (Wells) sleep in his (Whiting's) tent, and insisted upon doing so while Major WHITING was advising him against it. It was in this manner I offered to find him a tent to sleep in where he would be with a Black Republican—not as he says I did. Although the moment before, he had denounced Southern chivalry, and their institution of Slavery as a wrong and a curse, he became particularly incensed at this offer and invited himself into a stranger's tent. The next day, of his own accord, he came to my tent and begged me to say nothing more about the matter. His conduct and language for a long time afterwards

did not indicate that the fancies excited by the punch had
passed into settled hallucinations. On the contrary, when he
left the Camp and returned to York where my family lived, he
saw them, told them all about me, wrote an account of their
health, and even cautioned me not to speak unguardedly on political subjects "lest *some civilian* might take advantage of it to
injure me. When he wrote me at a still later period that he intended to accuse me of disloyalty for toasting the Southern
Confederacy, I did my best to deter him until I could convince
him, through Major WHITING, that he was in error. I knew he
was not a responsible creature and I could feel no enmity towards him. But all my efforts to reason with him only strength-
ened his mental delusion, and intensified the insane malignity
with which he had come to regard me.

MR. WELLS is not without that cunning which usually accom-
panies madness. Since his release from the Lunatic Asylum,
he has taken all occasions, in season and out of season, to make
his devotion to the administration conspicuous. But this is all
feigned, for, if what he said when the war began is any indica-
tion of his mind, he must be a confirmed secessionist. He
pushes his fortune and tries to win promotion by threatening
men with false accusations—always where he thinks it is his interest to do so—and several persons (among them his near relations) have been put in serious peril by his machinations. Thus
far he has been remarkably successful. It is a fact that this
Lunatic, so recently from the mad house, and seemingly unfit to
run at large, has been very recently appointed the Commandant
of the Navy Yard at Philadelphia.

When I was informed by Mr. Wells himself that he had made
this accusation, I did not think it necessary to send in a defense
for I had faith in the government of the Country which I had
served so long, and I believed that before any action would be
taken against me, I would be called upon for an explanation. I
certainly had no fear that the War Department would proceed
on the unsupported statement of a crazy man, when it was
known that there was a sane witness who could tell all about it
I however consulted friends and every one advised me that I

should not notice the allegations nor make any exposure of my accuser until it became absolutely necessary. I could not foresee that the necessity might exist without my knowing it.

I have made no assertions here which I cannot prove if an opportunity be given me, either by documentary or oral evidence. The letters, I refer to, are in my possession, the official reports are on file, and the witnesses will be forthcoming.

I do not suppose that either you or the President understood the nature of my case. Your action was grounded on the report laid before you, and I now respectfully request of you the privilege of proving before a Court of Inquiry, or properly authorized Court, that the report was made upon the false testimony of an incompetent and irresponsible witness, taken in a corner behind my back, and without the privilege to cross-examine. With these facts before you, I trust that, as an act of sheer justice to myself, an investigation will be ordered. If I shall succeed in this I will leave the rest with the utmost confidence in your hands.

I have the honor to be, very respectfully,
Your obedient Servant,
GRANVILLE O. HALLER,
(late Major 7th Infantry.)

# MEMOIR OF MILITARY SERVICES

OF

# MAJOR GRANVILLE O. HALLER,

## U. S. ARMY.

I was an applicant for the appointment of Cadet in the Military Academy at West Point, in 1839, but having turned my twentieth year, I received an invitation to appear before a Military board, which convened in the City of Washington, to examine the qualifications of young men who desired to be commissioned as Officers ; and having passed a satisfactory examination, I received from PRESIDENT MARTIN VAN BUREN, through the HON. JOEL R. POINSETT, Secretary of War, a Commission with the rank of Second Lieutenant in the 4th. Regiment of Infantry, from the 17th day of November, 1839. I had served in the Army, consequently, at the date of my dismissal, twenty-three years, eight months, and eight days.

In 1840, I joined my Regiment at Fort Gibson, a very sickly post, in the Cherokee Nation of Indians.

### THE FLORIDA WAR.

In 1841, my Regiment entered Florida the second time. My company formed part of MAJOR BELKNAP's column which explored and scouted the Big Cypress Swamp. In this expedition all the Officers and Men had to carry knapsacks, as the country was impracticable for horses or mules. Each one carried his change of clothing, blankets, and seven days' rations, and had to wade daily in water from ankle to waist deep, but mostly about twelve inches deep—in stretches of usually eight or ten miles—in the cold weather of December. I find honorable mention of my name, in this field, in SPRAGUE's HISTORY OF THE FLORIDA WAR—pages 360 to 376. On the 20th December 1841, the Indians in this swamp fired upon our column while in water three feet deep, killing several men.

In 1842, as Acting Adjutant of my Regiment, I served with the expedition under COL. WORTH which scouted the Wahoo Swamp, then crossed to the Palalikaha river, where his troops surprised HALLECK TUSTENUGGE in his camp with all of the women and children of the tribe about him, and obliged him to fight, to give time to the non-combatants to escape. The lodges, clothing and dried meats, etc. fell into our hands, after a sharp skirmish, in which they had several warriors wounded. This misfortune obliged Halleck to sue for peace, which was soon followed by the suspension of Indian hostilities. The Regiment was then sent to Jefferson Barracks, Missouri.

In 1844, my Regiment was ordered into Louisiana and encamped near Nachetoches, on the borders of Texas, as part of the "Army of Observation," as Mexico had threatened Texas with invasion on account of her negotiating terms of annexation with the United States.

In 1845, the 3d and 4th Regiments of Infantry became the "Army of Occupation" and took possession of St. Joseph's Island and Corpus Christi, Texas. I was here appointed "Brigade Major" of the 3d Brigade, a title now obsolete, as the duty is performed by the Assistant Adjutant General.

THE MEXICAN WAR.

In 1846, the "Army of Occupation" marched to the Rio Grande and encamped opposite Matamoros. I was here appointed the Commissary of 3d Brigade. At Point Isabella I was ordered to receive and receipt for all the subsistence stores, which the train of wagons would be able to carry to Fort Brown. Returning, the enemy met us at PALO ALTO, on the 8th of May, and disputed our passage, but had to fall back: on the 9th the enemy held a stronger position, and fought the battle of RESACA DE LA PALMA, and sustained heavy losses, and defeat. A large quantity of their subsistence stores, was captured, and placed in my charge. On the field, I acted as an Aid-de-Camp to Lt. Col. JOHN GARLAND, 4th Infantry, Commanding the 3d Brigade, and in his report of those actions, he has expressed his indebtedness to me for valuable assistance.

When the Army marched to Monterey, in addition to the duties of Commissary of 3d Brigade, I was charged with the duties of Quarter-master and Commissary to Gen. TWIGGS' Division. Immediately on our arrival before Monterey, I was ordered to take charge of all the subsistance that had been brought to that place, with instructions to be sparing in the issues, and by judicious distributions, protracted the subsistance until fresh supplies were received. I was kept on Commissary duty until Gen. WORTH's Division was withdrawn from Saltillo, to join Gen. SCOTT's column. Before embarking for Vera Cruz, Gen. WORTH directed Company Commanders, who were also doing Staff duty, to select one of the two duties which they preferred, and surrender the other. I thereupon retained command of my Company, and turned over my Staff duty to Lieut. GRANT, of my Regiment, now the distinguished MAJOR GENERAL GRANT.

At VERA CRUZ, Gen. WORTH's Division was charged with the construction of certain trenches, and my Regiment worked both night and day, then furnished guards for them. Our labors were incessant until the City capitulated.

At CERRO GORDO, my Regiment was part of the Reserve, but witnessed and participated in the success of that day.

The CASTLE OF PEROTE and the CITY OF PUEBLA fell without a blow, but the 4th Infantry formed part of the column sent to reduce those places.

In the Valley of Mexico, my Regiment participated in all the battles. At EL MOLINO DEL REY, I was one of the "Storming

Party," being selected as one of the officers to bring on the assault. In the CAPTURE OF THE CITY OF MEXICO, our last blow, my conduct seems to have met the decided approbation of my Superior Officers, and I may be pardoned, I trust, for presenting extracts from Official reports in regard to my services.

———

*Extracts from reports of Commanding Officers, in relation to the conduct of GRAN- VILLE OWEN HALLER Major 7th Infantry, in THE WAR WITH MEXICO, (then a Lieutenant of the 4th Regiment of Infantry,) extracted from THE EX- ECUTIVE DOCUMENTS, No. 1; 30th Congress, 1st Session: read December 7th, 1847, and published by the SENATE, to wit:*

From Gen. WORTH's report, speaking of THE CAPTURE OF THE CITY OF MEXICO, and dated at "Headquarters, 1st Division, City of Mexico, September 16th 1847." [See page 394.]

"I have again to make acknowledgements "to     *   .   *     *
S. SMITH, HALLER, and GRANT, 4th Infantry, especially;"

AGAIN:

From Lieut. GUS. W. SMITH's report while advancing towards the GARITA DE SAN COSME, one of the gates of the City, dated at "Engineer Quarters, City of Mexico, September 16th, 1847 [See Page 168, appendix.]

"*   .*   *     Lieutenants HALLER and JUDAH, of the 4th In- "fantry, and Lieutenant PICKETT, of the 8th, who were in "advance, gave me what information they had already acquired, "and rendered efficient aid in conducting the operations."   *   *

AGAIN:

From BREVET Col. JOHN GARLAND's report of THE CAPTURE OF THE CITY, dated at "Headquarters 1st. Brigade, 1st Division, Mexico, September 16th, 1847." ."[See Appendix, Pages 170 and 171."

"*   *   *.   I must not omit to call the attention of the " General to Lieutenant HALLER, of the 4th Infantry, who gave " evidence of courage and good conduct; his efforts were untiring "and crowned with good results; and, also, to Lieutenant

"GRANT, of the same Regiment, etc."    *    *    .    *    *

AGAIN:

From Major FRANCIS LEE's report of THE CAPTURE OF THE CITY, dated at "Headquarters Fourth Infantry, City of Mexico, September 16th, 1847". [See Appendix, Page 176.

"*    *    *    I detached Lieutenants HALLER and JUDAH,
"with A and C Companies, to support Major BUCHANAN; and,
" by his orders, they were advanced on the left of the road,
"through and over the houses towards the Garita."    *    *
"*    *    *    Lieutenant HALLER, with Company C. had been
"previously detached to another portion of the City on similar
"duty, which he executed in a satisfactory manner."    *    *
"My duty now requires that among all who behaved well, I
"name those who were most distinguished for their zeal and
"activity."    *    *    *    *
"*    *    *    and First Lieutenants GORE, SIDNEY SMITH
"(mortally wounded on the 14th,) and HALLER, and 2d Lieu-
"tenants GRANT and JUDAH, behaved with distinguished gal-
"lantry on the 13th, and 14th."    *    *    *
" Whilst I deem it proper to particularize the above named
" Officers, I cannot refrain from calling the attention of the Major
" General Commanding to the fact that there is not, nor has not
" been, a single Captain on duty with it.    This when a Regiment
" has behaved so well, and when its young officers have uniformly
" displayed such gallantry, should be taken into consideration in
"the distribution of those rewards which are the great incen-
"tives, etc."

EL MOLINO DEL REY.

From Gen. WORTH's Report, dated "Headquarters, 1st Division, Tacubaya,
September 10th, 1847," [See Pages 363-5-6.]

"*    *    *    when the assaulting party commanded by

"Wright, and guided by that accomplished officer, Captain
"Mason of the Engineers, assisted by Lieutenant Foster, dashed
"gallantly forward to the assault. Unshaken by the galling of
"the musketry and canister that was showered upon them, on
"they rushed, driving Infantry and Artillery men at the point of
"the bayonet. The enemy's field battery was taken, and his
"own guns were trailed upon his retreating masses; before
"however, they could be discharged, perceiving that he had
"been dispossessed of his strong position by comparatively a
"handful of men, he made a desperate effort to regain it. Ac-
"cordingly his retiring forces rallied and formed with this object.
"Aided by the Infantry, which covered the housetops (within
"reach of which the battery had been moved during the night,)
"the enemy's whole line opened upon the assaulting party a
"terrific fire of musketry, which struck down *eleven* out of the
"*fourteen* officers that composed the command and non-commis-
"sioned officers and men in proportion; etc.

*  *  *  *  *  *  *  *  *  *  *

"*  *  *  Commending the gallant dead, the wounded,
"and the few unscathed, to the respectful memory of their
"countrymen, and the rewards due to valor and conduct, I pre-
"sent the names of those especially noticed by subordinate
"commanders, uniting in all they have said, and extending the
"same testimony to those not named.  *  *  *  *

*  *  *  *  *  *  *  *  *  *  *

"ASSAULTING COLUMN.—Brevet Major WRIGHT, 8th Inf.,
"commanding, wounded; Capt. J. L. MASON, Engineers,
"wounded; Capt. E. MERRILL, 5th Inf., killed; Capt. A. CADY,
"6th Inf., wounded; Capt. W. H. T. WALKER, 6th Inf., wound-
"ed; Capt. J. V. BOMFORD, 8th Inf.; 1st Lieut. M. L. SHACKLE-
"FORD, 2d Art., wounded; 1st Lieut. C. B. DANIELS, 2d Art.
"wounded; 1st Lieut. G. O. HALLER, 4th Inf.; 1st Lieut. J.
"D. CLARKE, 8th Inf., wounded; 2d Lieut. J. F. FARRY, 3d Art.,
"killed; 2d Lieut. J. G. SNELLING, 8th Inf., wounded; 2d Lieut.
"M. MALONEY, 4th Inf.; 2d Lieut. JOHN G. FOSTER, Eng.,
"wounded."

AGAIN :

From Brevet Major WRIGHT's Report as commander of the storming party dated
"Tacubaya, Mexico, Sept., 10th, 1847." [See Appendix Page 165.]

The 2d company, composed of the 4th Infantry, was under
" Capt. WALKER, 6th Infantry, with 1st Lieut. HALLER."

" The conduct of all the officers and men on this occasion is
" worthy the highest commendation. Eleven officers, and a
"large number of the rank and file, were either killed or
" wounded."

AGAIN :

From Major FRANCIS LEE's Report dated "Headquarters 4th Infantry Tacubaya,
Mexico, September 9th, 1847," [Appendix, Pages 143–4.]

" The battalion, except a detail of 100 men for the storming,
" under Lieutenants HALLER and MALONEY, was formed, ect." * *

" It now only remains for me to designate those who gallantly
" distinguished themselves, and were most active during the
" day." * * * *

" First Lieuts. GORE and HALLER, especially mentioned to
" me by Major BUCHANAN ; * * * * * *

Then follows all the names of the officers of the Regiment, who
were present in the action, and immediately after he says : "It
" will be proper to state that 1st Lieutenant HALLER and 2d,
" Lieutenant Maloney, joined the battalion immediately after
" the charge of the storming party, and remained with it during
" the day."

CONTRERAS, SAN ANTONIO, AND CHURUBUSCO.

From Major LEE's Report of the series of "glorious victories" on the 20th, August,
dated at "Headquarters, 4th Infantry, Landrillera, Mexico, August 23d, 1847,"
[See Appendix Page 52.]

" I cannot too much commend the officers of my battalion.
" Their successful exertions are the more commendable as they
" were so few in number, and I beg leave, therefore, to mention
" their names."

Then follows all the names of the officers of the Regiment

present that day, among which will be found: "1st Lieut. G. O. HALLER commanding.Company."

AGAIN:

From Brevet Col. GARLAND's Report of the actions of the 20th August 1847, dated "Headquarters, 1st Brigade, 1st Divison, Tacubaya, August 23d, 1847," [See Appendix, Page 47.]

"* * * The 4th, Infantry at this moment rejoined me, "and Major LEE was directed to advance and occupy the "extreme right of our line. These movements were executed "under a heavy fire of cannon and musketry; our troops, how- "ever, continued to advance slowly, but steadily, through fields "of rank corn and over deep ditches. The battle field, from "the bridge head to the left of the enemy's line, was warmly "contested for about two hours, the musketry rolling without "one moment's intermission, etc."

For my services in MEXICO, I received two commissions by Brevet. The first one was the rank of *Captain* by Brevet, from the 8th, Sept., 1847, "For gallant and meritorious conduct in the battle of MOLINO DEL REY." The second was the rank of *Major* by Brevet, from the 13th Sept., 1847, "for gallant and merito- rious conduct in the battle of CHAPULTEPEC, Mexico." I have also been furnished with the resolutions of the Legislature of Pennsylvania, and my name has been inscribed in the journals of both the Houses, in compliment to my services.

### SERVICES ON THE PACIFIC SLOPE.

In 1852, my Company embarked on the U. S. storeship Fre- donia, sailed around Cape Horn, and after a seven months voy- age, reached San Francisco, thence sailed in a steamer to Fort Vancouver, Washington Territory, and shortly after, July 1853, was stationed at Fort Dalles, Oregon, then a Territory, a dreary, isolated spot, but since has become a thriving city, in consequence of the developments of the Gold regions to the East of it. In those days freight from Portland to the Dalles (one hundred miles) was $75.00 per ton : the ordinary necessities of a family, far exceeded an officer's pay : luxuries were scarcely to be had—eggs 12½ cents each, butter $1.50 per pound, contract price of Beef 27 cents per pound., etc. At that time it was indeed, mentally as well as pecuniarily, a great trial to be confined to a post so destitute of all that makes life agreeable.

## MASSACRE ON BOISE RIVER, AND MILITARY EXPEDITION.

In 1854, the family of a Mr. Ward, and other immigrants, were massacred on Boise River, about three hundred and fifty-five miles from the Dalles, by the Winneste Indians, a tribe of the great Shoshone Nation, under circumstances of the most atrocious barbarity.

The two companies then at Fort Dalles, were reduced by discharges and desertions to fifty-six soldiers . all told. I was dispatched with twenty-six of them to the massacre ground, there to chastise the murderers and give protection to the immigrants. The citizens of, and the immigrants at the Dalles, thinking my small force inadequate, formed a company of thirty-nine volunteers, followed after me, and reported for duty. At the Grande Ronde, (one hundred and ninety miles from the Dalles,) a few warriors of the Nez Perces, and Umatilla Indians offered their services to me, and were accepted. With this mixed force we invaded the usual haunts of the murderers, killed a few, and recaptured the clothing and other effects taken from their victims. With an old Indian, some squaws and children, captives, we brought up the rear of the Immigration. In the correspondence between Brig. Gen. JOHN E. WOOL, commanding the Department of the Pacific, and the then Secretary of War, JEFFERSON DAVIS, which was published by the U. S. Senate, I found the latter has expressed his approval, in strong terms, of my services and energy in this expedition.

## SECOND SNAKE INDIAN EXPEDITION.

In 1855, General WOOL organized a force of over one hundred and fifty men, and placed me in command, to further chastise these murderers. Returning to Fort Boise in the fishing season, we drove the guilty Indians from their fishing places on Boise and Payette rivers, then advanced some five hundred miles from Fort Dalles, and established a depot on the Big Camash Prairie, from whence we scouted the head-waters of Boise, Payette, and Salmon rivers, on the North of us, and to the Rocky Mountains and head-waters of the Missouri, on the East, and at Salmon Falls and along Snake river on the South. In this expedition we hung several of the murderers over the graves of their victims; in the mountains we hung and killed others, until we had destroyed as many warriors as they had killed of the whites, besides having captured women and children and old men. The remnant of the tribe fled in terror towards Humboldt river in California. In this expedition some of our horses had travelled at least seventeen hundred miles.

### EFFECTS OF GOLD DISCOVERIES.

About this time, the discoveries of gold by the employees of the Hudson Bay Company, near their trading post, Fort Colville, in Washington Territory, became well known, and caused many miners to visit that region; many passing from Puget Sound through the Klikatat and Yakima Country, and, in the latter, two or more miners were murdered. Having ordered my command to return to the Dalles, I proceeded in advance by rapid marches, and found a threatening state of affairs to exist quite close to Fort Dalles. The Indian tribes were sullen and hostile, and the Whites much excited. Major BOLAN, a highly esteemed citizen of Washington Territory, and Sub-Indian Agent in charge of the Yakimas, went to this tribe to counsel them for Peace and to get the murderers. He was assassinated. The Indians knew very well that if the death of their Agent became known to the troops, immediate war would follow. They therefore sent runners to inform their allies of their danger, and threw out scouts to observe the movements of the soldiers at Fort Dalles, and took every precaution to keep those Indians not disposed for war, from communicating with the white people.

### THE OREGON WAR.

The long absence of Major BOLAN from the Dalles, caused me to send an Indian Spy in the Yakima district to learn something about him. It was with difficulty he could get back. In the meantime an Old Squaw escaped through their lines and brought the news of BOLAN's assassination, and the collection of warriors from all the neighboring tribes to wipe out the White people. The information was confirmed in various ways, and it was duly communicated to the Commanding Officer of the District, stationed at Fort Vancouver. By this time the Infantry portion of my Battalion had arrived from the Camash prairie, and all the available force at Fort Dalles—making one hundred fighting men, divided into two companies, and one Sergeant Major, and one Commissary and Quartermaster Sergeant—total 102—having Captain (now Brigadier General) RUSSELL and myself commanding companies; Lieut. GRACIE in charge of the Mountain Howitzer; and Asst. Surgeon GEORGE W. HAMMOND, as medical officer—were held in readiness, with subsistence, for the command, prepared for the pack-mules, to march at a moment's notice. But this news brought me no orders to march.

Fortunately the Acting Governor of Washington Territory heard of the murders of the two Miners, and made a requisition for one Company of U. S. Troops to invade the Yakima Country from Fort Dalles and demand the murderers from that tribe. The Commandant of the District ordered me *to send a Company*, but knowing the peril, I took the responsibility of taking all my available force, and went in person. A consciousness of the danger induced me *to proceed with, not to send* this little band of soldiers, and I believe that the Adjutant General, of the U. S. Army, will bear me witness that I have never sought to avoid necessary danger, but have always encountered the enemy and used my humble abilities to the best advantage for my country.

## THE THREE DAYS FIGHTING.

The first night out my spy returned having escaped from the hostile camp and declared that Kamiarkin, the Yakima Chief, had collected more warriors than he was able to designate by numbers, and that a force double the size of my command would never be able to get back. We however advanced and on the fourth day, as we descended a hill to the bottom lands of Topinish Creek to encamp, we discovered the Indians taking position behind trees to fight. At the same time, a Chief on a distant bluff was making a harangue to his warriors, who replied to him with yells, and thus showed their positions and that they were not greatly superior in numbers. As soon as our mule train had come up and our rear was properly guarded, we attacked our adversaries and drove them off. During the action fresh warriors came up and showed themselves on the bluffs around us. At sundown perhaps six hundred warriors were in view but all retired during the twilight. Early the next morning the warriors surrounded our position but a few shots made them cautious, until they found our balls fell wide of their marks—we having only the old smooth bored muskets with spherical balls. In several instances war parties becoming more venturesome would crawl up very close to the knolls behind which our men awaited their approach, and would with stones construct what is now called rifle pits, to annoy our skirmishers when they exposed themselves, and these were driven off by bayonet charges.

Our position enabled us to see over the plain, and hourly fresh clouds of dust announced the approach of reinforcements to our foes. We had not rations enough to hold out until reinforcements from Fort Vancouver could join us, and it would have been as foolish as disastrous to attempt with my small force of foot soldiers to chastise or subdue the well mounted and active enemy before us. Prudence therefore made it my duty to return if practicable to Fort Dalles, where a properly mounted party would be organized to assist our efforts. Hence at night we retraced our steps to the top of the mountain near us, and allowed the men rest, and next morning fell back towards Fort Dalles, skirmishing with the Indians until nearly sundown. We lost five killed and seventeen wounded, and brought the wounded in safely, also the corpse of the gallant Commissary Sergeant MULHOLLAND, who fell in the last bayonet charge.

I may here introduce, I hope without impropriety, a letter from FATHER PANDOSY, of the Society of Oblates of the Immaculate Mary, of the Roman Catholic Mission in the Yakima Country, in regard to the number of Indians.

*To Major Haller:*

MAJOR : I had just returned from the Sound when you reached the Tapinnish. I found the Indians irritated in an excessive degree, I endeavored to calm their spirits, and for this purpose I sent expresses] to all the Camps to endeavor to induce the Chiefs to repair to my mission, representing to them that it was to their greatest interest to make peace. A good many who heard my message came, but the great majority were expecting that the moment had come to measure their strength with the white people, particularily the people of Kamiarken and the Klikatats, the great authors of the war ; the Klikatats have always made the Indians of this vicinity believe the Americans were cowardly and entirely inexperienced in the art of war, that in the war with the Shastas the Americans were defeated, and were obliged to employ their arms (those of the Klikatats) to make good their retreat, the Klikatats, I say, could not be restrained, and the spies sent by Kamiarken to examine the movements of the soldiers at the Dalles returned at the same time to the camp of Kamiarken and reported you were coming with a considerable force to ensnare in a net (*prendre dans un piege*) all the Chiefs. That you wished to speak them fair, and thus induce them to visit your camp, when you would seize and hang Te-i-as and his son, Owvrai and his son, Kamiarken, Shawawai and his son, Sklon and all the people who have influence. Some moments after, two or three Klikatats came into the camp of Kamiarken and announced your arrival at the "Assum," and (so close to them) that you had gotten in between the front and the rear of their party while advancing. These Klikatats came from Kamas Lake and Vancouver, and in their report they enlarged upon the report of the spies, saying that on their route they had been attacked several times, by 500 soldiers who had come from Vancouver to join you, and with the intention to increase the irritation of Kamiarken, they added that his great friend Tamiatas had been taken and hung.

On this news Kamiarken immediately sent expresses to all the Camps to assemble the men and direct them to advance to meet you at the Tapinnish. That you had been attacked by the Klikatats, who numbered four or five hundred men. They were at once reinforced with the people of Kamiarken, Shawawai and Sklon ; Owvria, who was farther off did not get the news so soon, and was later in directing his people towards the Tapinnish. If your position would permit you would have seen a continual procession the whole of Saturday and Sunday.

Knowing the small number of soldiers then at your disposal, the fierce rage in the hearts of some of the tribes, and the infinitely superior numbers of the savages, I did not think it possible you could execute so happy and honorable a retreat as that which signalized your return to the Dalles.

In the meantime all the warriors were marching to give you battle. I wrote you a letter by an Indian. They would consent to a peace if the Americans wished a peace and would grant a reserve on their own lands, and not exile them from their native country. But in case that their conditions were not accepted, they were resolved to fight to the last extremity, determined, even if they 'succumbed (these are their literal expressions) they would sooner destroy their wives and their children, than to have them fall into the hands of the Americans, who would gratify with them their infamous passions. Still, if the Americans and the soldiers desired a peace, they were willing ; if they preferred a war, they were also for war. Their numbers at this moment were fifteen hundred men, and if they wished it, they could soon have had two thousand men.

The number 1500 would appear to be exaggerated when one thinks that the Indians of the Mission had refused to take up their arms, and had retired to another country, but their numbers were fully replaced by the bands come, not only from the environs, as the Indians on the banks of the Columbia, the Walla-wallas, the Pelousas, Cayuses, Priests' Rapids, the Piskousas, but also the Chelelpams and the Spokans.

The best of the Chiefs, who wished for peace, and who was already distinguished for saving the lives of Americans, and giving them provisions for their road, was entrusted at the risk of his life, to carry you a common letter, but he did not overtake you until you were in the mountain and during the night. He camped near yours, because he feared the flag of peace, by which he approached you, might not perhaps be recognized, and in the morning on waking, you had continued your route to the Dalles. His horse was much fatigued, and he could not follow further. He returned to the Mission and assured me that you were beyond danger as the Indians were no longer pursuing you. This news rejoiced me greatly, and I could only attribute your safety to a special interposition of Divine Providence, who had been pleased to hear our prayers, for I believe it to be a moral impossibility that 100 soldiers could be able to resist 1500 Indians, determined to conquer or to die.

I have the honor to be, Major,

Your very humble and obedient servant,

(Signed) MIE CLES PANDOSY.

The above is a true translation of the meaning of my letter to Major HALLER.

MIE CLES PANDOSY, O. M. L.

The Commandant of the District being advised by courier of the defeat of my expedition, and the vast proportions that the war was likely to assume, called on the Governors of Oregon and Washington Territories, each, for two Companies of Volunteers.

## MAJOR GABRIEL J. RAINS' EXPEDITION.

Gov. CURRY, of Oregon Territory, believing that a respectable force sent into the hostile country would keep the enemy occupied at their own homes watching after the safety of their women and children, and thus save the White Settlements from rapine and murder, called out a Regiment and commissioned the present Senator from Oregon, General NESMITH, as the Colonel. But this commission being superior to the rank of the Major Commanding the District, the latter threw obstacles in the way of so large a force, apprehending the loss of command in the District. Some delay occurred and the winter weather overtook the troops in the enemy's country, and drove them back to the Dalles. It was not until the Acting Governor of Washington Territory had called out two Companies of Volunteers and made the Commandant of the District *Brigadier General of these two Companies* and such forces as should operate in his Territory, that the column was put in motion. Our forces consisted of about three hundred Regulars (among the officers, the present Major Generals SHERIDAN, ORD, and AUGUR, and Brig. Gen. RUSSEL,) and about five hundred Volunteer Cavalry, well mounted, marched through a dangerous gorge in the mountains into the Yakima Valley, and found a few Indians upon the opposite side of the river, evidently bent on annoying us. The Infantry was ordered across the river, but the water was so cold and swift that two men were chilled and unable to save themselves from drowning. Col. NESMITH then crossed with a troop of Cavalry and routed the enemy without a casualty, except a trifling wound to his horse. Another portion of the Cavalry had gone off in another direction, to forage, and was fired upon by the Indians and had a few men wounded.

Next morning we could see distinctly masses of the Indians on the "Buttes" at the mouth of Attanem Creek, only a few miles off, and some of the Braves came up quite close to our camp. Our General estimated the enemy at three hundred Warriors, yet these Braves disputed the passage at the "Buttes" until so late an hour that our command went into camp without dislodging them. Our General then invited the best marksmen to go out to the "Butte" in front, and have "a free fight" with the Indians on the hill, but our men were soon driven into camp in confusion. My company instantly sprang to their arms and covered the retreating party. I learnt from them that the Indians had come down into the timber on the river bank, and had opened a fire on their flank. Immediately my company charged the wood and followed the Indians up hill and drove them off the "Butte" without a casualty. As I advanced, I found Captain AUGUR's company supporting my movement. The Indians gave up the field for the night, but, early in the morning, attempted to resume their position on the "Butte." However they were quickly dislodged, and one of them was killed by a friendly Indian who had gone with me through all my Indian Campaigns. Soon after, snow began to fall, and our Campaign came to an inglorious end. This was my third Campaign, in the six months preceding, the first of which exceeded fifteen hundred miles of travel.

### KAMIARKEN.

The origin of the war in Oregon is not, I think, generally understood. KAMIARKEN, the principal Chief of the several bands, who live in the valley of the Yakima, should take rank with the most eminent Chiefs of the Red-men, known to fame, and is worthy the pen of a Prescott. A keen, far-sighted, and resolute Indian, devoted to his race, and most bitterly opposed to the encroachments of the White-man; he had kept strict watch over his dominions and never permitted a white man, excepting Catholic Priests, to obtain a foothold within his realm. He had travelled from Nation to Nation to warn them of their danger in letting the White-man stop to till their soil. At length the U. S. Commissioners called the several nations East of the Cascade Mountains together in Council to make a treaty and to fix upon contracted limits; the Red-men were told that they must give up many of the spots in which they had lived during their infancy and manhood. It was more than they could bear. They now recognized the wisdom of KAMIARKEN and turned to him for advice. He reminded them that in winter the snows covered the Cascade Mountains and the river froze over, so that the White-man on the West side of the Mountains had no means of coming to the aid of those in their country : therefore he advised them to begin to lay in supplies of ammunition and when the ice was formed, then "wipe" out every Whiteman who treads their soil. The White-man's treaty, he urged, was a hollow form, which, if it bound any one, only bound the Indian, for in the Willamette Valley the Red-men had made treaties several years before, but to that day they had not received one of the payments promised to them, and the Whitemen were now too numerous there to be driven off the Indians' land. The White-men gained time by signing the Treaties there ; he would sign the Treaty, lull the suspicions of the Whites, and get ready the materiel for war. The several Nations covenanted together to do so. The Klikatats around Fort Vancouver were in the League, and they sent messengers to the Indians on Rogue river, who also adopted the plan. A most terrible calamity was to fall upon the Whites in mid-winter. But the enthusiasm of KAMIARKEN's young men could not be restrained, and they revenged with death the insults of miners to their women. This brought on the war before the appointed time, and the Settlements were on their guard before winter came. The Rogue-river Indians, however, were only a few days behind in their blows, and when General WOOL arrived at Fort Vancouver, from San Francisco, he found the Governor of Oregon grappling in earnest with his barbarous enemy, leaving little for the General to do. Wounded in self-esteem, the General tried to convince himself it was no great war, and seems to have displayed an unworthy opposition to the measures adopted. KAMIARKEN fought and defeated my command, and he resisted Brig. Gen. RAINS' eight hundred men. But when he saw our numbers rapidly swelling with fresh troops, and no more hope for his poor Country, while Colonel WRIGHT was offering most tempting terms to his people, to get them to bury the Hatchet, he advised them to do so, and sent word to the Colonel that his "talk" was good and his people would accept it, "But as for me—I am KAMIARKEN still!" and he left his people, to dwell in the Buffalo Country, away from the White-man.

WHAT MIGHT HAVE BEEN DONE BY RECOGNIZING THE VOLUNTEERS.

It was customary for me in the fall of the year to make purchases in Portland for the winter, and when going down, Col. NESMITH requested me to deliver a letter to General WOOL asking for a Howitzer or two, and a few Artillerists, to be sent to the aid of the other portion of his Regiment, who were threatening the Indians, who had taken forcible possession of the Hudson Bay Company's Fort at the mouth of the Walla-Walla river. I had an agreeable interview with General WOOL at Fort Vancouver : he thought the Volunteers too numerous, that they drained the country of the materiel which he could use with better advantage in the hands of Regulars, and would create unnecessary expense. I suggested that the expenses had been already incurred, for which he could not be held responsible, and it would be desirable to make the very best use of the means which he found at hand, in order that the Indians might have plenty to do in guarding their women and children in their own country, and be thus prevented from attacking white settlements.

I stated my convictions that if we pressed the War party at Fort Walla-Walla with a large force, they would cross the Columbia river and seek refuge in the Yakima Country, hoping that the river would be a barrier to our pursuit. But the snow had already fallen on the Cascade Mountains on the West side, and on the hills to the North side, and was too deep for animals to travel through it, so there remained only the crossings of the

Columbia river, whereby the Indians could escape. Now if the Volunteers and Regulars co-operated, there would be sufficient troops to place a force upon every trail and pass leading into the Yakima Country. They could easily be crossed over the river and on a given day the whole force could advance, and the strength of this movement would be, that, the roads converging, would meet just where the enemy would be found, and the Warriors would be enveloped by this large force which must capture them, the women, and stock, and, bring the war to a close. The General seemed to be pleased, and inquired of me where I would construct a Fort if sent into the Walla-Walla Country, and subsequently advised me to drill my company at skirmishing, and get ready for a movement. The only objection which suggested itself to the General was the want of shoes, and the enfeebled condition of the horses that had just made three campaigns. But shoes and horses could have been supplied in time for this movement, if it had been desired.

### WHAT THE VOLUNTEERS ACCOMPLISHED.

The Howitzers were refused. The volunteers advanced on and captured the Fort, and after three or four days of fighting, defeated the Indians with considerable loss, and drove them out of that country, just in time for Governor I. J. STEVENS, of Washington Territory, (who was returning with a small party of Whites and Nez Perces Indians, from the Blackfoot Country, whither he had gone to make a treaty with that Nation,) to get through without being attacked by their large numbers. During the fighting PU-O-PU-O-MOX-MOX, an old Walla-Walla Chief, feared and respected by friends and foes for his shrewdness and resolution, being a prisoner, attempted to escape and was slain, and mutilations of his body, unworthy a civilized people, were perpetrated by a few individuals. The success of these Volunteers seemed to disturb the General. From this time he unsparingly denounced the Volunteers as if all had shared in the brutalities on PU-O-PU-O-MOX-MOX. He denounced the Governors and the people of the Territories, and styled the War as a "God send" to the people, who were all the while in imminent danger of the Tomahawk and Scalping knife. He even stooped so low as to misrepresent history connected with this war. He cautioned the public not to advance the Volunteers any supplies, and intimated that Congress would not reimburse the expenses of the Volunteers, if he could prevent it. The people fearing that the General's influence would retard the payment, if not prevent Congress from voting the appropriation, refused to furnish any more supplies. Yet supplies were indispensable, and the Quarter Master and Subsistence Departments were obliged to allow prices far above the market rates, to warrant the risks of the merchants as to getting their pay. The claims in Oregon and Washington Territories, growing out of this War, amounted to nearly $6,000,000. The General while trying to guard the purse-strings of the U. S. Treasury, did no other service than actually to swell the cost of things by a considerable per centage.

In "*The National Intelligencer*," of May 3d 1856, I found a letter, signed by JOHN E. WOOL, so full of falsehoods in regard to my three days fight, that I took the liberty of correcting them, and had a copy of my letter published in "*The Weekly Oregonian*," at Portland, in Oregon. I submit a copy to give an idea of his perversion of the history of that war.

CAMP IN THE VALLEY KIT-E-TAS, W. T., }
July 30th, 1856. }

*To the Editors of The National Intelligencer:*

GENTLEMEN : I have just read in your paper of May 3d, [tri-weekly,] a letter signed JOHN E. WOOL, dated April 2nd, 1856, addressed to you, and mainly occupied with denunciations of the Governors of Oregon and Washington Territories.

In that letter, however, occurs the passage hereto annexed, marked A, personal to myself, and injurious to my military character. The General therein asserts that I proceeded against the Yakimas, "*but without the precautions necessary against savage warfare.*" The specification in support of this charge is, that "*about sixty miles from the Dalles, on emerging from a deep ravine, he found himself, as he reports, confronted by 1,500 Indians,*" or as he elsewhere expresses it, that I allowed my command "*to have been drawn into a sort of ambush.*" [See letter of Nov. 3d, with Sec'y of War's report, Ex. Doc.]

The facts in the case are these : I was ordered to detail one *Company* for this service, and I deemed it *necessary to send out two Companies.* I further deemed it necessary to suspend the District Order which would have withdrawn LIEUT. E.

H. DAY, and 44 men of L Comp'y, 3d Artillery, to Fort Vancouver, and I directed that this Company and a Howitzer will be held "in readiness to march at any moment after the departure of the Infantry, and will be considered as the Reserve to the invading Battalion in case of necessity." These were the preliminary precautions ; and *en route* there were thrown out habitually the *Advance* and *Rear Guards*, and when in the timber the *Flank Guards*. What necessary precaution then has been omitted?

Now, on the 6th October last, when descending a very long hill in an open country,—yet Genl. Wool says, "*on emerging from a deep ravine*"—and approaching a stream whose banks were covered with oak trees and thick undergrowth, the advanced guard perceived the Indians in their front. At the moment a Chief showed himself and harangued his Warriors who replied with the War-whoop. These sounds of course exposed the position generally and the limited number of the Indians—they did not perhaps exceed 200 Warriors—yet the General says, *I reported that I was confronted by 1,500 Indians.* It happens moreover that I never did, in my reports, state the number, when at its maximum, to be 1,500 Indians. But I did notice the War-whoop in my report, and expressly stated that my Advanced Guard was drawn in, the troops deployed for action, and after the Rear Guard had closed up, the action was commenced—yet with these facts before him, Genl. Wool says *I allowed my command to fall into a sort of ambuscade.* The loss here was one killed and several wounded, and the General says : "*after losing two men killed and some thirteen or fourteen wounded, one mortally, he* [*I*] *escaped from his* [*my*] *perilous condition, &c.*"

The field was open to view like a chess board ; we could see War parties in the distance approaching, which swelled the numbers of the enemy considerably ; several moves of our adversary were checked, until finding my position guarded at all points, the real attack was developed. Capt. Russell's Company being on the left descended the hill, turned the right flank of the Indians in the brush, opened a fire upon them *en reverse*, and followed it up with a vigorous charge. The Indians fled and left the field in our possession. Darkness closed around us before the wounded were collected. We then advanced a mile and discovered, on ascending a height, that the Indians were not far off, as their voices were heard, apparently giving orders for an attack. We examined our ground, as well as the darkness would permit, and resolved to hold it ; we lay all night in readiness for their attack. Daylight, on Sunday, the 7th October, showed our position to be capable of defence, although destitute of wood, grass, and water, and decided me to await there coming events. We were surrounded very early in the morning by 600 or 700 Indians, and they continued to pour in, until evening, when I considered the number doubled. On this morning I wrote my first report, calling out my Reserve of 44 men, *and not* "1,000 *men to relieve me,*" as Genl. Wool has stated. The report was written *to be ready in case of disaster* [another precaution of mine] to apprise the command at Fort Dalles of our danger. Repeated charges with the Bayonet this day caused the Indian skirmishers to keep off so far as to render their firing comparatively harmless. Our loss was now 13 wounded and two dead. This evening I considered my command in imminent danger, and I resolved to extricate it by a night march. The troops retired in good order, the separation of the Rear Guard was immediately discovered and the Guide sent off to conduct it on our route, while we advanced to the summit of the mountain to halt there and rest the weary soldiers.  It was only after this that I ascertained the character of my guide.  Early on the 8th, we resumed our march towards the Dalles, and soon after a running fight ensued. I now dispatched my report, written on the previous morning, expecting the Express to explain the changes.  The timber concealed the number of Indians opposing us, but my second report did not justify the General's statement that "*with this small force* [40 effective men,] *he succeeded in making good his retreat, followed two days and nights by 1,500 Indians*" because I expressly stated that before sundown on this day, we again charged the Indians, drove them out of the timber, and after that they did not molest us.  Our total loss was 5 killed and 17 wounded—much greater than would appear from the General's statement, who draws the conclusion from his statement that, "*under the circumstances I did not consider such an enemy greatly to be dreaded.*"

Here are the main facts as briefly stated as a clear understanding of the circumstances, by the Reader, will permit, and they are substantially the same as those I submitted in my reports.  I have contrasted the facts with the distortions and exaggerations of General Wool, who "with an effrontery which even his white head ought not to protect from rebuke" adds, "*I think the number greatly exaggerated.*"  My estimate of the number, 1,200 or at most 1,400 Indians, does not materially differ from the statement of FATHER PANDOSY, of the Catholic Mission [whose letter is hereto annexed, marked B,] at the period of my retiring from the Sim-coo-a Valley, but the *Father* shows that even the General's 1,500 Indians falls far below the force ultimately collected to fight against me.

The General has in his letter voluntarily charged me, first, with exposing unguardedly "104 *Rank and File*" to an ambuscade of 1,500 Indians—a criminal neglect in a commanding officer— and afterwards expresses his convictions that I have exaggerated the number of Indians, therefore, in the second place, made a false report.  Even if the General's charges were true, the columns of a newspaper are not the proper place to arraign the offending officer.  The charges are very serious, then why has he not arraigned me for trial before a General Court Martial?  Here the General, I fear, has overshot his mark.  He has convicted himself either of gross neglect of duty in not causing an investigation and the punishment of the offender, or he has *gratuitously*, not to use a harsher expression, made charges to the injury of the military character of an officer placed under his command.

And, I regret to add, that, in looking around, I can find nothing to fix upon to exculpate or extenuate the General's conduct towards me.  I had made an application to him for a Court of Inquiry, long before his letter was written, which would have investigated the truth of my reports in relation to this expedition. He actually promised to grant the Court, *but it has never convened.*  And when I learnt casually that the General had sent a report of this expedition to Washington, at variance with my reports, and calculated I feared to prejudice the War Department in regard to my military capacity, I respectfully requested, in due form, a copy of his report, and he refused to grant it.  It was by the merest accident that I became aware, in this isolated region, of his unofficial attack upon me, before the public, in your paper. As General Wool's statements and charges have been published by you, I respectfully request that you will also insert this letter in the columns of *The Intelligencer*, and oblige

Yours truly,

G. O. HALLER,

Capt. 4th Inf'y., and Brevet Major, U. S. A.

## COL. GEORGE WRIGHT'S CAMPAIGN.

Col. WRIGHT with his Regiment, the 9th Infantry, but armed with the Minnie Rifle, a short time after Brigadier General RAINS' expedition, arrived at Fort Vancouver, and assumed command of the District. Gov. CURRY, of Oregon Territory, seeing an adequate force of U. S. Troops now ready to take the field, withdrew his volunteers.

The arduous services performed by my Company in the three expeditions of 1855, induced Col. WRIGHT to let it rest and garrison Fort Dalles, while he, in the Spring of 1856, marched with his available force against the hostile Indians. He had provided that one Company of his Regiment should garrison Fort Vancouver and another guard the Portage at the Cascades of the Columbia river, and as two other Companies were operating on Puget Sound, it left him only six Companies and a troop of Cavalry with which to erect several posts in the enemy's Country and also scout and chastise the Indians—he consequently had no soldiers to spare from his expedition. The transportation on the Columbia river being very limited, for the increase of business brought on by the war, it took time to get the Companies to Fort Dalles, and just as the Company designated to protect the Portage at the Cascades, was about to move, General WOOL made a flying visit in the Mail Steamer to Fort Vancouver, and finding the two Companies there took them off at once to Puget Sound, beyond Col. WRIGHT's control, without ascertaining what effect it might have on the Colonel's plans. To replace these losses in the Colonel's rear was to weaken and destroy his efficiency in the field. He therefore trusted the Portage to a Sergeant and a few men of the 4th Infantry and commenced his march. The hostile Indians, knowing the movement had commenced, sprang upon the settlement at the Cascades, and compelled the hitherto friendly Indians to join with them in killing men, women and children, and burning houses. One of the Steamers barely escaped capture. The soldiers defended their block-house and some families near by, and at the upper extremity of the Portage, all the citizens, who could, rallied in a large storehouse, and there made a gallant defence. As soon as the news reached the Dalles that night, Col. WRIGHT was notified, and next morning his command returned and took passage for the Cascades, where he encountered the enemy and soon routed them.

The several tribes around the Dalles still friendly, brought in their arms and proved the sincerity of their friendship by depositing them in my charge, and thus relieved from apprehension the minds of the White inhabitants. The Indians elsewhere, hitherto friendly, were surprised at this success against the Whites, and joined the War Party. Besides the serious loss of life and property at the Cascades, and detention and change of plan of Colonel WRIGHT's expedition, the Enemy became more confident and daring. Near the Nachess river, they were drawn up in position to oppose Colonel WRIGHT's progress into their Country. Their force had to be respected, and the Colonel thought it prudent to draw every available soldier from Fort Dalles to join him, so my Company again took the field. A Battalion of three Companies was placed in my charge, and with this force I accompanied him on his long march through the hostile Territory, north of the Dalles. Finally, I was left in the Kit-e-tas Valley to keep out the hostile Indians, until orders were received from General WOOL, in the fall of the year, for my Company to proceed to Puget Sound.

Col. WRIGHT, taught to believe that the Indians had been provoked, by the conduct of the Whites, into hostilities, offered the enemy *peace* if they would return to their homes and engage not to molest the White people, and he effected an understanding with several of the hostile tribes, as he retraced his steps towards the Dalles. But his experience afterwards must have convinced him that the Indians hated the presence of the

White-man, and designed to drive him from their country, for no sooner had the large nation of Spokane Indians the oppportunity of fighting our troops with a prospect of success, than they commenced a war. Brevet Lieut. Col. STEPTOE, with over one hundred and fifty mounted men of the Regular Service, was attacked by them, and after a severe fight was defeated, and this fine body of men was completely routed from their country, leaving some wounded to take care of themselves. As General WOOL "did not consider such an enemy greatly to be dreaded" it seemed as if Providence had come to my assistance and illustrated by comparison the General's mistake and the merits of my retreat.

I have dwelt longer upon the WAR IN OREGON, than the humble design of this pamphlet first contemplated. I intended to confine myself to my own services merely, but in this war my services were conspicuous, honorable, and attended with considerable danger, yet very few persons really know much of the history, except through Gen. WOOL's statements, and the role played by him being secondary to the Governor of Oregon, who was ex-officio Commander in Chief of the forces called out for the war within his Territory, and therefore galling to the ambition of a General, who was considered an aspirant to the high office of Constitutional Commander in Chief of the Armies and Navy of the United States. I may be wrong, but I have ascribed to this ambition the motive for his placing obstacles in the way of the Governor while endeavoring to subdue the ferocious enemies of civilization and progress, and it may account for the facts of history being distorted and obscured, and the services of his officers being maligned. Having, in my case, demanded a Court of Inquiry to investigate my conduct in this defeat, he made several attempts to convene one but it has never met, and two, of the three members, who were ordered to sit on the Court, are now dead. The reason for their not holding this Court has never been explained, but since that time General WOOL has published his letter of April 2d, 1856, and he has distorted the facts in my case to suit himself.

## FORT TOWNSHEND.

While I was in camp in the Kit-e-tas Valley, I was ordered by General WOOL, with my Company, to Puget Sound. I received orders, also, before leaving, from the Commandant of the Puget Sound District, Lieut. Col. S. CASEY, 9th Inf., to procure at Fort Vancouver the necessary building materials and implements, for constructing a Military Post, and to land my Company near the village on Port Townsend, in Washington Territory, and if I approved of the site already chosen for the Fort, to proceed to clearing the land of its timber, and construct quarters. After a reasonable time my Officers and Soldiers were provided with comfortable barracks, but the labor was severe and immense, to clear the timber away in a dense forest —trees from three to six feet in diameter, and nearly two hundred feet high—grade the ground, etc. Yet I had to superintend the work, be my own Pioneer in the woods, my own Architect to design the plans of the buildings, my own Quarter Master and Commissary of Subsistence, and do the duty of Lieutenants, for those promoted to my Company had not then joined. Mr. GEORGE GIBBS of Washington Ty., came to my assistance and relived me very much. The change from the excitement of the field service to constant hard labor was a trying one to soldiers. The discovery of rich gold fields, on Fraser river, offered strong temptations to the soldiers to desert to British Columbia. There never was a time when more vigilance was required of one Company officer, and I am sure that no officer ever gave more faithful services to his Country than I did at Fort Townshend.

### SAN JUAN ISLAND.

The Department of Oregon was formed in 1859 and assigned to Brig. Gen. HARNEY. He soon altered the face of things, directing Posts, that had just been constructed, to be abandoned, and new ones to be established elsewhere. Ignoring the instructions of the Secretary of State, MR. MARCY, to the Governor of Washington Territory, to abstain from further exercise of authority on San Juan Island until the water boundary between the United States and the British Possessions should be determined by competent authority—and COMMISSIONERS were then engaged in adjusting this very line—he sent the Company from Fort Bellingham (just abandoned,) to take possession of San Juan Island and suspend British authority there, and substitute that of the United States. Captain PICKETT, Commanding, issued a proclamation to this effect in orders. The Authorities of British Columbia were highly incensed at it, and took measures to collect all their available force near the Island, and might have plunged the two countries immediately in war, but for an insignificant incident, and, as they had five formidable War Vessels in the waters of British Columbia, they might have suspended, if not destroyed our immense commercial interests on the Pacific Coast, before the Authorities in Washington could be apprised of the trouble—for there was then no telegraph across the Continent as now.

The incident alluded to, was the arrival of our mail bringing European news, but, particularly, the battle of Solferino. The British officers first heard of this battle from us, as their mails had failed to arrive. It occurred to them that MR. DALLAS, our Minister in England, might there have adjusted the boundary question, and that General HARNEY might have received instructions from Washington to occupy the Island. This idea prevented them from taking forcible possession of the Island, and before they had obtained positive information to the contrary, GENERAL SCOTT had arrived, and solved the controversy, by allowing an equal number of British Marines to occupy the Island, and British subjects to obtain protection by application to their own Magistrates, until the proper Authorities had mutually agreed to a boundary line and the ownership of the Island.

The news of British preparations for hostilities soon reached Fort Steilacoom, and the Steamer "Massachusetts" being then in port, awaiting orders, the Lieutenant Colonel Commanding the District, immediately dispatched me with my Company, (and a small detachment of Infantry, for the protection of MR. CAMPBELL, the United States Boundary Commissioner at Semiahmoo, against depredations of Northern Indians,) with instructions to advise with Captain PICKETT and, if he required aid, to land my forces and assume command : to observe the proceedings of the British Navy, and to keep Headquarters of the District advised of important occurrences : but the ostensible reason, for appearing in the Archipelago, was orders to search the Islands for Northern Indians, and remove them beyond our frontier. I reached the harbor on the 1st of August, and found Her Majesty's Steam-Corvette "TRIBUNE" at anchor, and soon after the "SATELLITE" and "PLUMPER" arrived with a strong force of British Marines and Sappers and Miners, on board, from Fraser river. I communicated my instructions to Captain PICKETT, and awaited coming events. The British Officers questioned me closely, about the news by the mail and of Solferino, and they gradually quieted down, so that I felt at liberty to scout for Northern Indians. As soon as General HARNEY heard of the British preparations, he sent all his available force on the Columbia river over, and directed Lieut. Col. CASEY to take them, and his command at Fort Steilacoom, to the support of Captain PICKETT. I was soon after ordered ashore to assist in fortifying the Island, but the arrival of GENERAL SCOTT broke up the Camp, without completing the defences.

IMPORTANCE OF A STEAMER, FOR U. S. TROOPS, ON THE SOUND.

While examining the shores of the Islands, in the Archipelago, I received a call from the Citizens of Whatcom, by an Express-boat, stating that a party of Nooksahk Indians, painted and armed, taking advantage of the withdrawal of the Troops from Fort Bellingham (one mile off), had entered the town and threatened the lives of Citizens, and were resolved upon releasing an Indian Chief held in prison, and actually shot one man, when the Citizens resisted it, by returning their fire and killing four or more Indians. I hastened to that town, landed my men, and by a march of twenty-five miles struck the river between the point where the tribe had assembled to receive their dead friends, and their homes above, so that they could not pass up the river without my consent. They were astonished to find troops between them and their lodges. They had not had time to think how they should revenge this loss. They received my demand with submission, gave up the Ring-leaders for punishment, and the difficulty there subsided.

A few days time for those Indians to have brooded over their loss, would most probably have involved the settlement, at Bellingham Bay, in murder and rapine, but the unexpected presence of troops in the heart of their country was so wonderful to them, as to drive all thoughts of revenge out of their " hearts." The Steamer undoubtedly saved a war.

### FORT MOJAVE.

In August, 1859, my Company was sent to San Francisco, and on arriving there, was ordered to Fort Mojave, on the Colorado river, (of the West,) in New Mexico, over three hundred miles from San Pedro, in California, from whence all our supplies were hauled overland in wagons. This Post has been regarded as the very worst in the United States. In the midst of an arid desert, extending a hundred miles to the East and West, located on a barren *Mesa*, overlooking the bottom-lands, there was nothing in common with the familiar scenes we met with everywhere else, but the Cotton wood trees on the river bank, and a garden requiring constant irrigation. The heat of Summer is most intense, and wind storms charged with heated sand and dust sweep over the spot for days together. No attempt had been made before my arrival to raise potatoes, or cabbages, and we obtained these, grapes, and other fruit, from Los Angelos, in wagons—a distance of two hundred and eighty-five miles.

While at this post, the United States Astronomical party made their observations to determine the longitude of the point where the 35th parallel of North Latitude touched the Colorado river, a short distance below the Fort. During their stay the Secession movement was inaugurated. MR. MOWRY, the U,

S. Boundary Commissioner, had sent to the Fort a large number of young gentlemen, who favored the movement and discussed the matter freely, and, in their letters to the newspapers of San Francisco, giving the *on dits* of Fort Mojave, they made repeated mention of my devotion and attachment to the Union "under all circumstances," as they expressed it. Maj. Gen. WINFIELD S. HANCOCK, being Quarter Master at Los Angelos, in his letters, kindly kept me advised of the progress of this movement, and he too is aware of my sentiments, from my letters.

Officers have served faithfully in such isolated posts as FORTS DALLES and MOJAVE, and put up with great inconveniences and even sufferings; but they have endured them the more willingly from the knowledge that in after years such services have always been taken into consideration, greatly to the advantage of those who remained faithfully at their posts. But in my case, the sacrifices, the hard and faithful services, even the loyal sentiments entertained by me, count as nothing : I cannot get even a hearing. Is this right after nearly twenty-four years of faithful service? I appeal to SENATORS and LEGISLATORS of the U. S. Congress, and ask if this is proper?

In 1861, Brig. Gen. SUMNER assumed Command of the Department of California, when he ordered Fort Mojave to be evacuated, directing me to send the property and the Company of the 6th Infantry to Los Angelos, and to proceed to San Diego with my Company over land, making the march over four hundred miles. I reached San Diego in June, and the following November embarked my Company for New York, and thence proceeded to Washington City, and arrived there on the 19th of December, 1861.

I found I had been promoted a Major of the 7th Infantry, but several Companies of this Regiment were on parole, and as I preferred active service, sought duty with the Army of the Potomac, and was assigned to Brig. Gen. ANDREW PORTER's Staff, and appointed by him an Assistant Inspector General in the Provost Marshal General's Department. While around Washington, I made several efforts with MR. STANTON and Brig. Gen. MARCY, Chief of Staff, to get the 7th Infantry exchanged, with the expectation of having the command of them in the field. Their exchange seemed so probable that I declined opportunities where I might have obtained the rank of Colonel and Command of a Volunteer Regiment. The Southern Confederation, however, placed obstacles in the way, and I entered the Peninsular Campaign without them. While the Army lay at Harrison's Landing, I obtained from GENERALS McCLELLAN, FRANKLIN, and BARRY, strong letters of recommendation to Gov. CURTIN, as to my qualifications for Commanding a Regiment, having previously had a conversation with the Governor, who expressed a preference for Regular Officers to Command Volununteers; but, he said, the War Department positively declined letting him have them. I obtained the necessary permission, and soon ascertained that political recommendations were worth much more than the very best certificates of qualifications for the duty, and dropped the matter, for I have never sought any advancement on my political merits, and have never troubled MR. LINCOLN's Administration, in any way, for promotion.

As the Army of the Potomac left Fortress Monroe for Yorktown, Va., I had the honor to be appointed COMMANDANT OF GENERAL HEADQUARTERS, and in this capacity served during the whole of the Peninsular and the Maryland Campaigns; was retained by GENERALS BURNSIDE and HOOKER, until my health, (an obstinate *impetigo*, irritated by exposure to the weather) obliged me to seek in-door duty.

In the Peninsula, I had under my Command five Companies of Volunteers, whose duties were to keep faithful watch over the tents of the several officers at General Headquarters and the important papers in their possession, particularly, when the officers were absent from camp discharging their duties; also, to escort the General Headquarters' wagon train when on the march and prevent the official papers from being captured. This small Battalion performed its duties most faithfully and efficiently, and on several occasions it was held in readiness to engage with the enemy, when near the James River, in the march from the Chickahominy.

This Battalion and a few troops under the Provost Marshal

General, were all that were left with General McClellan on his arrival at Alexandria, Va., and scarcely had he encamped, before I was ordered to report to Brigadier General Haupt, in charge of Railways, with all the available troops at General Headquarters, and was sent to Fairfax Railroad Station, to protect the supplies there for General Pope's Army. At the time, this Army was falling back towards Washington, and the wounded were sent here for removal, in the cars, to Alexandria. My command was busily employed for three days at this camp, and, in the meantime, General McClellan was ordered to Washington and required my services. Although there had now been collected over one thousand volunteers in the camp, exclusive of the General Headquarters' troops, yet most of them had just been defeated and felt unsafe in that camp, and I felt apprehensive they would retire if an opportunity permitted. In an interview with General Pope's Assistant Adjutant General, I gave him my views, and he thought I ought to stay, and I did not leave until I had ascertained that the enemy during the night had passed along General Pope's right towards Leesburg, and a sick soldier came into my camp who had just come from the intrenchments at Mannassas without seeing a rebel soldier. With this information I felt at liberty to depart, but learnt subsequently, that, in a few hours after, the volunteers withdrew, leaving some employees at work loading cars with the surplus provisions which were ordered to the rear. I had indicated, soon after my arrival, to General Haupt that we had sufficient supplies in that camp, and requested him to send us empty cars to enable us to dispatch the wounded promptly, which he did on learning my reasons. On our return to Alexandria, we found that the General Headquarters had removed, and we followed on to Washington, but in a few days General McClellan was again placed in Command, and advanced rapidly towards Lee's Army, then at Frederick, Md., and THE BATTLES OF SOUTH MOUNTAIN AND ANTIETAM soon followed.

In this Maryland Campaign, Capt. Welden's Company of 19th Regiment of Regular Infantry, and the 93d New York Volunteers were placed under my charge, as the General Headquarters' Guard, and rendered efficient aid. The Army Corps, when they had fallen back to Washington, did not get time to refit and replace the articles lost in their retreat, and before entering Virginia again, it was but proper that their necessary wants should be supplied. This occasioned some delay, but gave offi- cers a fine opportunity to instruct their commands. I superintended the drills of Gen. Headquarters' Guard,and had the satisfaction of seeing the men improve rapidly, and the officers feel pride in acquiring a knowledge of their duties. Subsequently, these officers expressed, in a substantial form, their appreciation of my services, by presenting me through the Colonel of the Regiment, JOHN S. CROCKER, a very handsome sword, silver hilt, having a silver and also a bronze scabbard, a serviceable sword belt, a crimson sash and several sword knots. These were delivered, in the presence of Major Generals BURNSIDE, HOOKER and SICKELS, Brig. Gen. BUFORD and many other Officers of the Army of the Potomac, accompanied with interesting remarks on behalf of the donors. On the silver scabbard was inscribed :

Presented to
MAJOR GRANVILLE O. HALLER
7th Inft. U. S. A. Commanding Gen'l Head Quarters
by the
Officers of the 93rd N. Y. Volunteers,
Head Quarters' Guard, Army of the Potomac,
As a token of regard for his social qualities as a
Gentleman and his Military ability as an Officer.
Camp near Falmouth, Va., January 1st, 1863.

Crossing the Potomac, at Berlin, Md. the Army again resumed the invasion of Virginia, and while marching successfully towards Culpepper, taking possession of the gaps in the mountains as we advanced, we were told that we might expect a battle in four or five days, and that it should be on ground of our General's own choosing. The army was in high spirits, and had never before been in such perfect fighting order, never better drilled, and never felt more confidence in their ability to defeat the Rebels in an open field. But suddenly, at midnight, a Bearer of dispatches arrived from Washington with orders for

General McCLELLAN to turn over the command to Major Gen. BURNSIDE. The news astounded all! The blow fell upon the army. of the Potomac, and they gave unmistakable evidences of their grief. Thinking only of his country's success, Gen. McCLELLAN encouraged Gen. BURNSIDE to take the command, and offered to remain and assist him in the approaching battle.

Gen. BURNSIDE however changed the whole plan of campaign, and expected to reach Richmond by the Fredericksburg route. He arrived before this city, but found his pontoons were not on hand, and the delays here were fatal to his plan. Before he crossed, the enemy had time to throw up fortifications, and his Army was defeated with terrible loss, without gaining a single advantage to console us for the misfortune. Croaking and jealousies, the bane of an Army, could now be recognized, and Gen. BURNSIDE's usefulness was destroyed. Gen. HOOKER succeeded to the command, but before he was prepared to cross the Rappahannock, I had left the field on account of my health. The failure at Chancellorsville enabled Gen. LEE to invade Maryland and Pennsylvania the second time.

THE SECOND INVASION OF PENNSYLVANIA.

I was in York, Pa., when the advance of the Confederate Army entered Chambersburg, and a telegram from Governor CURTIN informed the Citizens that the Enemy were expected to advance on Harrisburg on the next day. Next morning I hastened to that place and reported to Major Gen. COUCH, Commanding the Department, in hopes that I might be able to assist him in organizing for the defence of that Capital. The General immediately placed me on duty as an Extra Aid-de-Camp on his Staff, and sent me into York and Adams Counties to direct military operations in that District.

I hastened to York, where a Committee of Safety had been organized, and proposed that all the people be aroused and called upon to defend their firesides.—To get as many persons to enlist in the " six months' service," or " for the emergency" as would repair to Harrisburg, and class the rest into Companies of " HOME GUARDS," having men from sixty to forty-five in first class; from forty-five to thirty in second class; and from thirty to fifteen in the third class, so that age might exclude none. Each one to report what fowling piece or other arms he might have, and have his name registered with description of the arms. Thus to have the actual force that could be relied upon organized, and to have the arms and ammunition ready. But I was particularly urgent upon the Committee to organize a command of efficient *Scouts* and also of *Pioneers*. The former to go to the front and keep advised of the enemy's movements and communicate them to the Headquarters, and the latter to obstruct the roads, especially the mountain roads. I directed that trees should be felled into the roads from the one side, so as to allow a wagon barely room to pass along on the other side of the way, then hack the trees on this side until nearly ready to fall over the road, so that in a few minutes they might be felled and the road be made impassable to the enemy's Cavalry and Artillery.

This latter party had not been organized, when I endeavored to get the members of the 87th Penn. Vols., who, having escaped from the disastrous affair at Winchester, Va., by various routes, had returned to their homes in York and Adams Counties, and were ordered by me to rendezvous in York, and were in charge of their Lieut. Colonel. On the 23d June, I telegraphed the Committee of Safety to explain my plan to Lieut. Col. STAHLE and say he was authorized to obstruct the roads towards Carlisle, particularly the Conewago mountain roads, but received the following telegram :

"YORK, June 25th, 1863.

" *Major Haller, Gettysburg :*

"Lieut. Col. STAHLE has received orders from Gen. MILROY. We requested
"Gen. SCHENK that he and his men be retained here. The reply was Maj. Gen.
"MILROY has orders to report with all his command at Baltimore, and the troops
"at York must join him.
　　　　　　　　　[Signed]　　　　　　"JOHN GIBSON,
　　　　　　　　　　　　　　　　　"Sec'y. of Safety Committee."

The object here was to prevent the enemy from invading York from the direction of Carlisle, but in like manner, it would prevent the enemy reaching Carlisle from York. This work was not attended to, and the failure is of importance, inasmuch, as Maj. Gen. EARLY marched his Confederate Division, when he evacuated York, by this very route to Dillsburg. It is a matter of History that the arrival of this Division on the battle ground at Gettysburg, during Wednesday's fighting, to the right but considerably in rear of Gen. HOWARD's line, obliged him to change his line and fall back to Cemetery hill, which resulted in the enemy capturing about 3,000 of our men. Had the obstructions been attended to, the command of Gen. EARLY would have been delayed for hours, perhaps lost all of Wednesday, and these barriers would have made an important detention in favor of the Army of the Potomac.

Having made preliminary arrangements in York, and studied the grounds about Wrightsville with a view to defend the Columbia bridge, I hastened to Gettysburg to make some necessary arrangements there. I arrived just in time. The next morning, June 20th, many droves of horses came into Gettysburg from the neighborhood of Waynesboro, and the Riders gave out exaggerated statements of the enemy's numbers and their movements. I was induced to ride out to the Monterey House, on the mountain top, to get accurate information. I ascertained there that a force of about one hundred Rebel Cavalry were then at the foot of the West slope of South Mountain, searching for horses. I called upon the farmers around to turn out and block up the roads by felling trees, which they did in good earnest. However next day, before a party of armed Citizens sent from Gettysburg had reached the Monterey House, a small party* of the enemy's mounted Infantry on foot, leading their horses, worked their way up to that place through the woods, driving in our pickets, who had pistols only, while the mass of them passed northward and crossed the mountain at Cold Springs, which had not been obstructed, and swept through the Western end of Adams County, by the "Tract" road. They observed Captain BELL's troops advanc-

---

*Mr. Phillips of Waynesboro, reported to me that this body of the enemy was at least three thousand strong, for he had seen them with his glass. Showing how liable respectable witnesses are to deceive themselves.

ing, but part of his force was concealed, so they could not tell his number—he having then the available force I could collect at the moment, (about twenty-five City Troop, and fifteen Adams County Cavalry,) with which he was sent to reconnoitre. The enemy was taken by surprise and recrossed the mountain, taking those at Monterey with them, and without pausing a moment at Fairfield, notwithstanding Professor JACOBS of Gettysburg gives them a two hours' stop at that village, in his little·· book entitled "Notes of the Rebel Invasion."

From this time until June 26th, Captain BELL's available force, including the City Troop, were kept in constant motion, and all performed their duty with commendable zeal and ability, and kept me, and therefore Maj. Gen. COUCH, fully advised of the movements of the enemy. These troops were all that rendered me any assistance. The 26th Reg. Penn. Vol. Militia was, indeed, sent to my aid, but I would gladly have passed over their misfortunes, but for the remarkable statements made by the Rev. M. JACOBS, Professor of Mathematics and Chemistry in Pennsylvania College, at Gettysburg, who has assumed to give the Reader of his "NOTES" a true account of the great battle fought there and of my preliminary efforts to arrest the march of the Confederate Troops.

### THE TWENTY-SIXTH PENNSYLVANIA MILITIA.

A young gentleman, connected with the Christian Association, who professed to have been with this Regiment, and who was represented to me as a Clergyman, very coolly informed a near relative of mine, that Major HALLEN had laid a trap by which this Regiment would have fallen, as Prisoners, into the hands of the Rebels, or have been cut to pieces, but for the Colonel's assuming responsibility and leading the Regiment out of the trap. And Professor JACOBS has suggested that my conduct was owing to incapacity for the position I then held, or to the indifference I felt for the result of our arms. He then informs his Readers that soon after uttering the remark that " He (I) would first fight the Rebels, but after the war, the Administration." I was dismissed for "disloyal conduct and the utterance of disloyal sentiments," and "the golden opportunity for efficient preparation" to resist the enemy was allowed to pass away.

Now as I had proposed to arm the people and oppose the Enemy with deadly weapons, the logical deduction, from his quotation, is, that after the war I intended to fight the administration with deadly weapons, for which I was dismissed by the War Department. And the Reader's mind now being poisoned against Major HALLER he tells how I ordered the 26th Regiment "although contrary to the earnest remonstrance of Jennings, Colonel, &c." to the front and how the Colonel "seeing the trap into which he had been led" extricated his men, after having nearly all of his pickets captured, forty in number, first, and then losing one hundred and twenty more of the regiment near Hunterstown on his retreat. In this statement, I have endeavored to present fairly the substance of two Professing Christians' statements, especially the substance of Professor JACOBS' language in his book.

I will therefore give a few points to aid the Reader's judgment:

1st. Gov. CURTIN and Gen. COUCH fully believed that EWELL's Corps of Confederate troops, was advancing on Harrisburg to capture the Capital of Pennsylvania, and very few people, if any, in the State, doubted this.

2d. No one would have supposed that Gen. EWELL would, while threatening Harrisburg, send off a single Division to spend the 4th day of July in the City of Philadelphia.

3d. It was to be expected that the Enemy would send out small parties to collect Provisions and Forage from our Citizens' granaries, gather up Horses and Cattle, and obtain information of the movements of our Forces.

4th. It was my duty to protect, as far as the means at my hand would permit, the Counties of Adams and York from these little incursions.

5th. The only means at my hand on which I could rely, was Captain ROBERT BELL's enlisted men, then forming a Company, having about thirty-three private horses, owned by the soldiers, and about seven horses taken by the Deputy Provost Marshal from Deserters or Stragglers from the U. S. Army, found at Gettysburg—say forty in all ; and Ensign SAMUEL J. RANDALL's Detachment of about forty-five young gentlemen from Philadelphia, of the 1st City Troop, well mounted, who paid their personal expenses, and served without being mustered into the Military Service.

Besides these, Major CHARLES McL. KNOX, of the 9th N. Y. Vol. Cavalry, an experienced and valuable officer, who was an invalid, and on sick furlough, but hearing that his native hills (he was born near Gettysburg) were invaded, and knowing every spot of ground about those hills, hastened to Gettysburg and offered me his services. Also Captain SAMUEL L. YOUNG, an Attorney-at-Law, of Reading, Pa., who had acquired experience on the Staff of Maj. Gen. KEIM, and whose assistance was also valuable.

The 26th Penn. Militia came and went attended with misfortunes. I will now give the official history as far as I have it, of this regiment.

General COUCH's written instructions were as follows :

"Colonel JENNINGS will use his best efforts to hold the country, harrass the "enemy,—attacking him at exposed points or falling back in order—and ad-"vancing his force or part of it, 'making flank attacks etc., doing everything in "his power to weaken, mislead the enemy and protect the country."

I did not ask for a Regiment, for I believed all General COUCH's troops would be required for the defence of Harrisburg. But he telegraphed : " Would it do to send a Regiment of Infantry "to Gettysburg ?" To which I answered ; " Please send a " Regiment, it will restore confidence and rally the people to "take arms." The third day after, I received the following note :

"SWIFT RUN HILL, June 24th 1863.
"Major G. O. Haller,
"DEAR SIR : We have met with an accident at this point ; the cars hvaing "run off the track. We sustained no injury further than damage having been "done the track and several cars, I shall camp here and await your orders."
Yours Respectfully,
(Signed) "W. W. JENNINGS,
"Colonel Commanding 26th Regiment Pa., Militia."

I authorized him to impress teams to bring up his baggage, and march to Gettysburg, if the railroad was not repaired when he would be ready to move, next morning.

At this time, Captain YOUNG had voluntarily posted himself at Cashtown to collect information and superintend the scouting on the mountain. At $8\frac{1}{2}$ o'clock P. M. June 24th, he dispatched a note saying : "I advanced two miles—saw rebel Cavalry." He gives a report that there are Infantry, Artillery, and Cavalry on the top of the mountain and adds : "the report seems to be reliable."

This note arrived about 11 o'clock at night, when I telegraphed General COUCH, and arranged with Major KNOX, to reconnoiter in force, and communicated the necessary orders to secure an early start in the morning. This done, I then dispatched the following note to Col. JENNINGS, Commanding 26th Pa. Militia.

GETTYSBERG, Pa., June 26th 1863. }<br>(2 o'clock A. M.) }

Colonel : Get the cars ready to return to Hanover if possible on receipt of this : if not, impress wagons and *be ready* to fall back in a moment's notice.

The enemy in force, Artillery, Infantry, and Cavalry have already possession of the mountain pass and no doubt intend marching here, perhaps to day.

By Command of MAJOR GEN. COUCH.

June 25th. During this morning, General COUCH telegraphed me, "Let me hear the result of your reconnoissance of this A. M." To this I answered, as follows : "Rebels hold the mountain but have not advanced. Our Cavalry, under Major KNOX, are cautiously advancing and observing. No other official report. Unreliable report says they are fortifying."

Major KNOX, it seems, approached within two hundred yards of the top of the mountain, when he was fired on by Infantry. In his report he says : "I think it very suspicious "that I have not found their *Cavalry*, and my opinion is that "the rebels will move by another road than the turnpike "and that their Cavalry will precede them, hence I will scout *all* "the roads etc." Major KNOX not finding any Rebel troops elsewhere, inferred that this party was a "Flanking Brigade."

This was important news. It indicated that the rebel forces were securing the mountain passes in the direction of the Army of the Potomac, to prevent their line of retreat as well as communication being cut off, by our crossing the mountains. All the information gathered this day only confirmed this hypothesis. I telegraphed to General COUCH this day ; " Our information indi-" cates that rebels have evacuated Hagerstown, even Waynes-" boro', going North. Suppose our opponents to be a flanking " brigade." As soon as General COUCH, on the night of the 24th, . received 'my telegram that the enemy was on the top of the mountain, he telegraphed back as follows : " It would be well if " you could find out what the Rebels are doing. Can't you get " some Riflemen on their flanks in the mountain ?"

On the afternoon of the 25th of June, believing the Enemy would not advance, I endeavored to conform to the General's suggestion. Accordingly I wrote as follows :

DEPARTMENT OF THE SUSQUEHANNA, }
GETTYSBURG, PA., June 25th, 1863. }

*Col. W. W. Jennings, Commanding 26th Penn. Militia :*

COLONEL : Can you raise a party of *reliable* riflemen who dare go into the mountain, on the flank of the rebels, to discover what they are doing and harrass them ? Please report quickly how many can be raised.

By command of MAJOR GEN. COUCH.

Colonel JENNINGS promptly replied as follows :

" SWIFT RUN HILL, June 25th, 1863.

*"To Major G. O. Haller :*

" DEAR SIR : I will send one hundred (100) men in charge of Capt. LEMUEL " MOYER—who will march directly and report to you for further orders."

Believing that Colonel JENNINGS had more than one hundred old soldiers—two years' men and nine months' men—in his Regiment, I congratulated myself on having their assistance, taking it for granted he would send no other troops for the important service proposed. I also wrote to the Colonel to " come " up. The cars have been ordered to your camp, at 5.30 " o'clock,-A. M., to bring your command to this place (Gettys-" burg). Please be ready and hasten the loading, so as to be " here before the hour for the passenger cars to depart. The " Regiment will encamp about three miles from town, towards " the mountain, in supporting distance of the Sharp Shooters.

" By command of MAJ. GEN. COUCH."

The Colonel had due notice of the destination of his Regiment in writing thus early, but he did not remonstrate in writing or otherwise to my knowledge. Strange to say the provisions for this Regiment were not, for some reason, brought on with the men, and they were without rations. The one hundred men had no suppers, nor anything to subsist upon in the mountains. Late as the hour was (near midnight) through the assistance of members of the Committee of Safety, some rations were procured. Captain MOYER having now his Command provided for the march, called for instructions. Our guides were there, who knew a **by**-path to the hill, at Moonshour's house. This hill is precipitous towards **the** Chambersburg pike and becomes a formidable position to the enemy on the turnpike road, who, being in a gorge between the mountains, would suffer heavily, if not be thrown into confusion, by a handful of determined men. I soon indicated to Captain MOYER, on the map, the route, and position to be in before daylight, and what was expected of his men.

I was distressed to learn from Capt. MOYER, after all the pains taken to get the right kind of men, that the Old Soldiers had been left in Camp: that a simple detail had been ordered from each company of "ten men for detached service:" that the men he had brought knew nothing of deploying or acting as skirmishers: that some did not even know how to load, for the officers had not yet had a chance to drill them. Of course the expedition was deferred. But these were the "Picked men" of Professor JACOBS—the *reliable* riflemen who dare go into the mountain on the flanks of the Rebels, to discover what they are doing and harass them, of the Colonel Commanding the Regiment.

On the 26th June, the Regiment arrived and Capt. BELL conducted it to the Camping ground on Marsh Creek. Before Capt. BELL left the Colonel, in his Camp, he received the first news of a Rebel advance, which he communicated to the Colonel, saying he would go forward and see what it might be. Having seen a party of Rebels advancing very slowly, he returned to the Infantry Camp, from whence he wrote me as follows: "To MAJOR HALLER. Camp of Regiment. I have seen the "advance of the Rebs just beyond New Salem—probably 50 or "100. (Signed) R. BELL, Captain." This hundred of the enemy was all that we knew then to be advancing. But the Colonel expressed a want of confidence in his men, saying if he only had his old regiment he would feel safe : then asked how he could get away from his position. Captain BELL replied that the road to Gettysburg was open : the Colonel answered that the enemy would overtake him before he got there. Captain BELL then inquired which way he wanted to go : the Colonel answered Harrisburg or York, when Captain BELL pointed out the way.

Capt. BELL again rode to the front, perhaps too miles, to get another look at the party of rebels advancing. Having again seen them, he came back, but Col. JENNINGS and his Regiment were retreating by the road he had pointed out, and were half a mile off already. On the way to town, Capt. BELL met my orderly going out with a message to Col. JENNINGS to come in, when the Captain informed him that the Regiment had left.

Now we had reason to believe that, while the main body of Rebel troops would hold the mountain pass, they would send into the valleys just such parties to gather horses, etc., and if I had been in Command of that Regiment, I should have considered it my first duty to ride to the front with Captain BELL, and see that the scouts took positions to ascertain the possible number approaching, with a view to make proper disposition of my Regiment, to meet them, or retire, as the case required. But the Colonel, without attempting to look after the fifty or one hundred Rebels, hurried off without informing me of his unexpected movement, and without giving any orders to his detachment which he had left in Gettysburg to guard the cars, which had by this time been forwarded by the Railroad Company, with his provisions. The slow and cautious advance of the Enemy, would have allowed the Regiment ample time to reach Gettysburg unmolested, and as his guard to the subsistence stores—about 40 men—who did not leave until after I did, came away without loss, I have no reason to believe that his Regiment would have lost a single man.

Now, the facts in the case show that Col. JENNINGS chose his own line of retreat, moved off entirely upon his own responsibility, and that he had marched a half mile from the position in which I placed him, while the enemy were yet a few miles off, without the loss of a single man. As a matter of course, then, what happened after this time is due entirely to Col. JENNINGS' management, who took upon himself the responsibility.

This Regiment marched several miles unmolested, but then came upon a marauding party of fifty or sixty Rebels that were gathering horses between Mummasburg and Hunterstown, and here it was that the Regiment met the Rebels first and last, and Professor JACOBS says they lost 120 men, but none I believe killed or wounded. The suppers which the Regiment missed the night before, and which they much needed on this evening, refreshed the hungry soldiers of Major Gen. EARLY's Rebel Division.

Having gathered up the Public Arms, and accoutrements, Brass Gun, etc. at Gettysburg, and sent them to Hanover, where the public property in my charge was held ready for removal, I retreated to that place and had the stores promptly removed, then ordered the troops to proceed to York.

The citizens of Gettysburg, at my request, had organized a Committee of Safety, and some of the members feeling great interest in the Military proceedings, spent much of their time at my quarters. These gentlemen were made acquainted with the information I had obtained from time to time, and the object of my several movements, and consequently, are at this date important witnesses as to my loyalty and my zeal for the service. It happens that the writers of the several letters, which I subjoin, are well known for their Republican Sentiments, and their opinions must be conclusive to all who know them. It is but justice to Professor JACOBS to say that he has retracted all his offensive remarks as to my conduct, loyalty and zeal.

Mr. McCONAUGHY's zeal for the success of the Union cause has been so strongly marked by his acts, that his testimony, in my favor, is the more strong as he would have been the first to take alarm at any act of disloyalty on my part. He writes :

GETTYSBURG, October 29th, 1863.

SIR : Having been constantly in intercourse and actively co-operating with Major G. O. Haller, while on duty here in June last, as aid to Major Genl. D. N. Couch, Commanding the Dept. of the Susquehanna—I cheerfully state, that, Maj. Haller was constant and earnest in the discharge of his duties, at this post.

Not only was there neither act nor expression proceeding from him, in any manner suggestive of disloyalty, but on the contrary his whole bearing and conduct here was characterized by zeal and activity as an officer. From my intimate knowledge of all that was transpiring, and the facts which furnished the basis for his action, I was strongly persuaded, that, his proceedings in advancing the 26th Regiment, (Col. Jennings'), were justified by the information derived from Cavalry reconnoissances, and furnished him by the officers in charge of the scouting operations.

With the limited forces at his command, Major Haller's whole actions impressed me with the conviction, that, he was seeking earnestly to do, all that he could, for the public service and the defeat of the enemy, and thwarting its movements.

As a citizen who felt a very intense interest for the success of the Arms of the Union and the rout of the Rebel forces ; and, keenly alive to any thing, however slight, which might betray a want of loyalty in any one with whom I might be thrown in contact, I have no hesitation in thus strongly giving expression to the impressions made upon me in my intercourse with Major Haller.

Most respectfully and truly,

D. McCONAUGHY.

## R. G. McCREARY and DAVID WILLS, Esquires, write :

GETTYSBURG, PA., Oct. 28, 1863.

*Maj. G. O. Haller :*

SIR : It affords me pleasure to state that as a member of the Committee of Safety, appointed at a public meeting of the citizens of this town, in June last, I was frequently at your quarters, and had knowledge of the efforts made by you to arrest or retard the progress of the rebel army on the borders of our county, by organizing the citizens as "Home Guards" and otherwise, and to testify to the zeal and earnestness manifested by you on the occasion, and that, so far as my observation extended, your conduct and conversation were uniformly such as became a loyal citizen and an officer of the United States Army.

Very respectfully yours,

R. G. McCREARY.

---

GETTYSBURG, PA., Oct. 29, 1863.

*Major G. O. Haller :*

DEAR SIR : I fully concur with Mr. McCreary in the substance of the foregoing letter. In addition I take the liberty to add that I told you I was sorry to see that the Democrats of our town did not attend the meeting called b

Committee of Safety, which meeting was held at your solicitation for the purpose of making arrangements for the organization of Home Guards for border defence. You suggested that you were of that political pursuasion and wished to meet some of the prominent men of that party to endeavor to pursuade them to unite in the efforts making to repel the invaders, and that they should fight the rebels first and after that they could attack the administration in a legitimate and constitutional way. I know that you made every effort to bring about a concert of action here for the purpose of organizing the Town and County for border defence.

I remain yours truly,
DAVID WILLS.

Captain ROBERT BELL, of Gettysburg, also writes:

GETTYSBURG, PA., Oct. 29, 1863.

*Major G. O. Haller :*

MAJOR : It affords me great pleasure to be able to testify to the earnestness and zeal you displayed in June last, during the Rebel invasion. Having access to your room at all hours day and night, and in frequent *confidential* conversations with you, I have no hesitancy in saying you did every thing you could do as a loyal officer of the Government with the small and inaffective force you had at your disposal to retard the advance of the Rebels east of the South Mountain, and that I had no reason to doubt your loyalty whatever, and was very much surprised to hear of your being dismissed from the service. If I can be of any further service to you it will afford me great pleasure.

I am yours most obediently,
ROBERT BELL,<br>Capt. Adams County Scouts,<br>(now Co. B, 21st P. V. Cav.)

On the afternoon of the 27th of June, the scout on the Abbottstown road came in, reporting about 100 Rebel Cavalry advancing rapidly towards York, and no other troops could be seen approaching by that road. As the Adams County Cavalry, by purchases, and by impressing horses, had become mounted, this troop now numbered over 60 men, which with the "City Troop" exceeded 100 men. Through the foresight and system of discipline, adopted by Surgeon PALMER, U. S. Vols. in charge of the U. S. Hospital in York, I found about 225 Convalescent Soldiers armed and equipped for service; besides a company of volunteers ("Patapsco Guards") in charge of the public buildings and property; and a few of the 87th Penn. Volunteers. With this force, I marched to the West end of York to keep off me. marauding parties, until the hospital stores (in very large quantities,) might be removed, and the rolling stock, at the Depot, could be sent away. This movement was not appreciated by the Citizens, who, apprehensive that a collision might subject the town to the vengeance of the enemy, believed it would do the inhabitants much injury. However, information soon came that the whole force, which invaded Gettysburg, was marching to York, and would be there that night. This scout had even been in General GORDON'S presence, and had, in writing, his assurance that if there was no resistance offered at York, all the private property would be respected. He assured the scout that he, himself, had over 3,000 men—and the scout thought GORDON'S Brigade was by that time only three miles from town. This scout, MR. FAUQUIER, was vouched for, by MR. SAMUEL SMALL, as an honest man, and what he stated should be believed. On this state of facts, I withdrew the troops to Wrightsville, leaving only a few Cavalry men in front of York, to observe the approach of the enemy, and report the time of their occupation. They remained until 8.30 o'clock, P. M., but no enemy appeared. Next morning, at 10 o'clock, the Division of Major Gen. EARLY entered, and quietly took possession, drawing his supplies through the civil authorities of York, and, during his stay, preserved most perfect order, strictly prohibiting his men from molesting the inhabitants or committing depredations.

Wrightsville presented a melancholy spectacle. Hundreds of loaded wagons were awaiting their turn to cross the Columbia Bridge. The rolling stock of several of the Railroad Companies was crowded together. The Locomotives and cars had to be hauled by horse power across the bridge, and the means to transport these were only those animals used for the ordinary demands of trade at that place. I called on DR. EVANS, President of the Bridge Company, who, at my request, dispensed with tolls, and the wagons then crossed lively, and once in Columbia, their horses were impressed to haul over the rolling stock, and thus property of immense value was promply secured.

Colonel J. G. FRICK, Commanding the 27th Penn., Volunteer

Militia, was posted in front of Wrightsville with his Regiment, to whom I turned over the troops from York. Tools were procured that night, and early next morning rifle pits were thrown up, and the approaches carefully examined, to station troops in effective positions to defend the bridge from any raid sent to destroy it. But our evil genius, GORDON's Brigade, with Cavalry, and Artillery, again presented itself, and while getting into its position and reconnoitering our lines, quite a number of shots were exchanged, and sufficient numbers of their force were displayed to show the hopelessness of a defence of Wrightsville, wherefore the troops were withdrawn, and the span of the bridge, (which had been carefully sawed apart, excepting the arches, which were charged with powder, to blow them to peices and let the span fall into the river) was ordered to be destroyed. The powder failed to do its work, and the enemy was seen approaching the bridge when Colonel FRICK, ordered it to be set on fire. General EARLY said in York, that, if the bridge had not been set on fire, he would have been in Lancaster the next (Monday) morning. Colonel FRICK's opinion of my conduct and loyalty on this occasion is expressed as follows :

POTTSVILLE, PA., Oct. 23d, 1863.

*Major Granville O. Haller :*

DEAR SIR : It affords me great pleasure to say that during the time we were associated together in the military service of the country at Columbia and Wrightsville, you manifested great zeal in behalf of the best interests of the country, and was indefatigable in your efforts while aiding me to make such dispositions of my small force as would enable us to repel an attack of the rebel horde that marched against us from York. At no time did I hear you utter a disloyal word or sentiment. I believed then as I believe now, that your activity and anxiety to thwart the enemy was prompted by the purest and most patriotic motives. Certainly no one of my command questioned for a moment your patriotism or your sincerity.

My orders were to prevent the enemy from crossing the Susquehanna at or near Columbia at all hazards ; and when the propriety of destroying the Columbia Bridge was being discussed, you joined with me that the best interests of the service—the safety of the Capital of the State, as well as the preservation of Railroad communication between that point and Lancaster and Philadelphia, demanded its destruction.

In conclusion I have only to say that your conduct met, as it deserved, my approbation, and I have yet to hear a word of disparagement from those with whom you were associated.

Very respectfully, your Ob't. Serv't.,     bANGN T/

JACOB G. FRICK,

Late Col. 129th Pa. Vols.,

and Col. 27th Pa. Vol. Militia.

Gen. COUCH then directed me to give my attention to the defences of the Susquehanna, to visit the several fords and see that proper defences, (rifle-pits and abattis,) were constructed to harass the enemy, if not defeat them, in any attempt to cross the river. When this danger had passed, he relieved me, and while in York writing out reports of my proceedings at the several towns, and my reconnoissances at the several fords of the Susquehanna, I received on the 28th of July, in reply to my enquiry of the Adjutant General, whether I should repair to my regiment? a telegram from Major ROBT. WILLIAMS saying, that, " By Special Orders No. 331, of July 25th, 1863, you are dismissed the service, by order of the Secretary of War."

## OBSERVATIONS.

The principal object, in the foregoing pages, has been to present the evidences of *my* LOYALTY *to the Constitution and the Union* and to vindicate *my conduct and sentiments* to my Countrymen. But these pages will do more : they will furnish materials for serious consideration for the Thinking portion of the community.

My *dismissal*, from the U. S. Army, would be of little consequence, if it were not for the principles involved—principles which have been established and respected by every Administration from the organization of this Federal Government, except the present one. My dismissal is a part of the history of the times, and every Patriot may read and consider its tendency, with profit.

The facts presented in these pages contain internal evidences of the destruction of those fundamental principles which have heretofore regulated at least the administration of the War Department. It will be difficult to shut out from one's mind the evidence that we are now governed on the principle that "MIGHT MAKES RIGHT" to the exclusion of those principles which relied on their INHERENT WISDOM AND JUSTICE for the support and approbation of the American People. It will be difficult to believe otherwise than that the Secretary of War is conscious that his charges of "DISLOYAL CONDUCT AND THE UTTERANCE OF DISLOYAL SENTIMENTS" cannot be sustained, and will not bear a moment's investigation; else why does he mutely refuse me an investigation of his direct charges against me? It seems equally clear, that the Secretary of War has dismissed me for a reason, or reasons, which he is unwilling to announce to a Thinking Community, and therefore takes pains not to write and not to grant anything touching my case—not even to allow me to get a copy of *the report*, or more properly speaking, *the proceedings* of Colonel HOLT, the Judge Advocate General U. S. Army, whose examination of the "INFORMER" in private, and remarks on the statements, caused my dismissal. And here I will cite the act of Congress, approved April 10th, 1806, commonly called the "*Rules and Articles of War,*" which, so far as the authority of Congress goes, is "the Law of the Land" to-day. It reads:

Art. 90. Every Judge Advocate, or person officiating as such, at any General Court-Martial, shall transmit, with as much expedition as the opportunity of time and distance of place can admit, the original proceedings and sentence of such Court-Martial to the Secretary of War; which said original proceedings and sentence shall be carefully kept and preserved in the office of said Secretary, *to the end that the persons entitled thereto may be enabled, upon application to the said office, to obtain copies thereof.*"

It is manifestly the spirit and the letter of the Law that an officer should have a fair trial, and be furnished with a copy of the proceedings. If the Department were honorably administered there would be no occasion for concealment, and the refusal to investigate creates a suspicion that there is something radically wrong in the action of the Department.

The Reader may consider whether the War is any longer NA-

TIONAL? The whole country was aroused and united by the Resolutions offered by MR. CRITTENDEN, and adopted by Congress, that the existing war was to restore the Federal Authority in the States now in rebellion, and, when this is accomplished, the war is to cease. It was not to interfere.with any of the rights inherent in those States. In this the Northern States were as one. But are they one now? Are we not now subject to the dictation of a party occupying a section only of the whole Union? Is that party trying to preserve the Union as it was,, or going to reconstruct it? Is the administration trying to preserve the Union as it was, or using all its energies, its power, patronage, and its reputation, to keep alive this sectional party? Let the Patriot ponder on these things well! Is, or is not this a partisan War? What officers in the Army are tabooed? Have any officers in the military service been dismissed for taking the stump in favor of the Administration, or the party which supports it: or for exerting themselves at elections in behalf of the Party which elected MR. LINCOLN to power? Have, or have not, officers, with the highest grade in our army, set an example of *stumping* a State?

But the most remarkable thing which is connected with my dismissal, is, *the tribunal* which has brought it about. The INFORMER is one CLARK H. WELLS, a Lieut. Commander of the U. S. Navy: the PROSECUTOR is Colonel JOSEPH HOLT, who had the case all to himself: and the JUDGE and EXECUTIVE is EDWIN M. STANTON. And, these were devoted friends (?) of the Democratic Administration while MR. BUCHANAN dispensed the public patronage. But they are now devoted friends of the Administration, or " the Government."

Of the latter two, it is generally understood, they were competitors for the office vacated by MR. CAMERON, Ex-Secretary of War, and the influence of GEN. McCLELLAN at that time, with the President, obtained for MR. STANTON the Port-folio. Such partiality and kindness, with most gentlemen, would have created a feeling of indebtedness, and a disposition to support to the utmost such a benefactor. We might naturally expect cordiality and harmony in the councils of the Secretary of War and

General-in-Chief. But public sentiment had recognized in GEN-ERAL MCCLELLAN a Military Genius—the military operations in all quarters were prosperous, and victories marked our path—and all successes were ascribed to him. The power and abilities of the Secretary of War seemed lost to public view. This did not suit MR. STANTON. He soon took upon himself the Command-in-Chief of the Army—he soon took away from MCCLELLAN a part of his Army, and he saved Richmond from MCCLELLAN's grasp! Yes! and if MCCLELLAN's generalship had not saved his Army on the Chickahominy Creek, MR. STANTON's Generalship would have given the Southern Confederation such a victory as would have secured the recognition of their Independence in Europe.

As for Colonel HOLT, we find a still less amiable disposition. As the blood hound follows the track of his victim and never lets up until he is destroyed—it may be said of him, he never lets up until he has accomplished the ruin of him he wishes to destroy. It is not likely that he will forget or forgive GENERAL MCCLELLAN for using his influence to his [Col. HOLT's] prejudice, when seeking MR. CAMERON's place—nor will he forget any of that General's particular admirers.

I have before me a letter written by Col. HOLT dated "Washington, Nov. 30th, 1860," which pleads so strongly for the South, that no political views of mine should be offensive to him. The Colonel writes:

"We shall soon grow up a race of Chieftains who will rival the political bandits of South America and Mexico, and who will carve out to us our miserable heritage with their bloody swords. The *masses* of the people dream not of these things. They suppose the Republic can be destroyed to-day and peace will smile over its ruins to-morrow. They know nothing of civil war. This marah in the desert of the pilgrimage of nations has happily been for them a sealed fountain. They know not as others do of its bitterness, and that civil war is a scourge that darkens every fireside and wrings every heart with anguish. They are to be commiserated, for they know not what they do. Whence is all this? It has come because the pulpit and the press, and the cowering, unscrupulous politicians of the North have taught the people that they are responsible for the domestic institutions of the South, and that they can be faithful to God only by being unfaithful to the compact which they made with their fellow men. Hence those Liberty bills which degrade the statute books of some ten of the

Free States, and are confessedly a *shameless* violation of the Federal Constitution in a point vital to her honor. We have here presented from year to year, the humiliating spectacle of free and sovereign States, by a solemn act of legislation, *legalizing the theft of their neighbors' property*. I say THEFT, since it is not the less so because the subject of the despicable crime chances to be a slave, instead of a horse or a bale of goods.

From this same teaching has come the perpetual agitation of the slavery question which *has reached the minds of the slave population of the South*, and has rendered every home in that distracted land insecure. This is the feature of the irrepressible conflict with which the Northern people are not familiar. In almost every part of the South, miscreant fanatics have been found, and poisonings and conflagrations have marked their footsteps. Mothers there lay down at night trembling beside their children, and wives cling to their husbands as they leave their homes in the morning. I have a brother residing in Mississippi, etc., etc. He has replied to me at much length, and after depicting the machinations of the wretches to whom I have alluded, and the consternation which reigns in the homes of the South, he says it is the unalterable determination of the Southern people to overthrow the Government, as the only refuge which is left to them from these insupportable wrongs, and he adds : " On the success of this movement, depends my every earthly interest—the safety of my roof from the fire-brand, and of my wife and children from the poison and the dagger."

· I give you his language because it truthfully expresses the Southern mind, which, at this moment, *glows as a furnace in its hatred to the North because of these infernal agitations.* Think you that any people can endure this condition of things ? When the Northern preacher infuses into his audience the spirit of assassins and incendiaries in his crusade against slavery, does he think, as he lies down quietly at night, of the Southern homes he has robbed of sleep and the helpless women and children he has exposed to all the *nameless horrors of servile insurrection?*

I am still for the Union, because I have yet a faint hesitating hope that the North will do justice to the South, and save the Republic before the wreck is complete. But action to be available must be prompt. If the free States will sweep the Liberty bills from their codes, propose a convention of the States, and offer guaranties which will afford the same repose and safety to Southern homes and property enjoyed by those in the North, the impending tragedy may yet be averted, but not otherwise. I feel a positive personal humiliation as a member of the human family in the events now preparing. If the Republic is to be offered as a sacrifice upon the altar of African servitude, then the question of man's capacity for self-government is forever settled. The derision of the world will henceforth justly treat the pretension as a farce, and the blessed hope which, for five thousand years, our race, amid storms and battles, has been hugging to its bosom, will be demonstrated to be a phantom and a dream."

\*    *    *    *    *    *    *    *    *    ?    *

[Signed,]    ·        J. HOLT.

As for Lieut. Commander WELLS, he can produce evidence to

prove himself a Secession Sympathiser—a Democrat—a Republican and exquisitely loyal to the. present Administration, as it may suit his interests.

Notwithstanding he reported me on the 3d of March, 1863, to the Secretary of War, for uttering in his presence, on or about the 15th of December, 1862, such "disloyal sentiments" as to "call forth a severe rebuke" from him and to cause him to leave my tent,—all of which he assures the Secretary ; yet in January and February, between these dates, he kept up quite a pleasant correspondence with me, from the Philadelphia Navy Yard, assuring me that "no one can doubt his loyalty"—"when we are engaged in a deadly struggle to sustain our Government, I would sacrifice my son." [The poor little boy! Harry, his only son, was only seven years old! and thinks of sacrificing him, while he is safe at the Navy Yard at Philadelphia !] "I regard slavery as a curse to our country and the cause of this hell-born rebellion."—"Were it not that I had been away a year in the South Atlantic Squadron, and for the sake of my family, I would prefer going to sea in these exciting times, although my naval friends tell me that I have done my share. I think not, for I believe that no officer can do too much to assist in crushing out this sinful rebellion."

But, for this glowing loyalty, he had obtained his price ! For as long as he had been a Democrat, he assured a political acquaintance that "The Democrats have never done anything for me : but see what the Republicans are going to do—why they are going to send me to the Philadelphia Navy Yard."

Even a solemn oath is no obstacle to this officer, for after he had sworn on the Holy Bible to the new oath of allegiance, he declared to a visitor that he "had just performed the most painful act of his life—that he had been compelled to take the oath of allegiance, or be dismissed from the service, and that his necessities had made him do this violence to his views regarding the war then commencing."

And in •a letter before me, written with his own hand, he says : "I should not be surprised if I should be obliged 'to turn my sword into a ploughshare.' I would rather do that than be called upon to use it against my countrymen."

And while with the South Atlantic Squadron, he there solicited the command of a leaking vessel knowing that it must soon be sent home for repairs; and soon after landing in the North, he solicited and obtained the command of the Navy Yard at Philadelphia; and has ever since escaped active service against the Southern Confederacy.

These are not my assertions, they are the statements of different gentlemen, whose veracity will not be questioned, and who can make oath to their declarations. Yet this MR. WELLS is the INFORMER in my case: all three, in this tribunal, are known to have entertained sentiments at variance with those they now profess, yet make no allowance for a difference of opinion in others.

In the foregoing pages I have given a synopsis of my military service for nearly twenty-four years, with a few extracts from official reports as to my conduct. I have been in a great many important engagements with Civilized, and with Savage foes, and have been honored with strong expressions of commendation from my Superior officers. I have seen the printed list of the officers recommended for Brevets, for services in 1862, and found my name had been submitted to the Senate, for the Brevet Commission of Lieutenant Colonel. I believe my services have uniformly been satisfactory. Notwithstanding I have been on many well-fought battle fields, and have on all occasions faithfully discharged my duties;—notwithstanding I have endured great privations, hardships, and dangers:—notwithstanding I have aided as far as laid in my power, to restore the Federal authority in the States now in rebellion:—I have been expelled from the Army overwhelmed with whatever of infamy it is possible for MR. STANTON to heap upon me, and he has exchanged my knowledge and experience in War, for a person who must enter the Regular Army at the bottom of Second Lieutenants, and then learn his profession. It is true Mr. STANTON can appoint one, whose friends may bring him more influence to support his designs, but this cannot make the Army more efficient. And, in this way a designing man, with, an Army so immense as ours now is, may prostitute the office of

Secretary of War to procure influence, until his power is sufficient to trample the Constitution under his feet.

Is it then DISLOYAL to examine into, and speak of the conduct of members of the Administration ? On this point, I will quote JUDGE PEARSON of the Dauphin District of Pennsylvania, who is well known for his Administration sentiments, or to use the language of the newspaper before me " a double-dyed Republican." In a charge to his Grand Jury on the subject of *disloyalty,* he says : " Do not misunderstand me on this point : men " have the most unlimited right to condemn, and if you please, "to rail at the National Administration, and to object to the " manner in which it conducts public affairs. * * * *

" Parties will always exist in every free country, and wheth- " er men will sustain or oppose a particular Administration " is one in which there should ever be the most perfect freedom " of opinion. * * * * * * * *

" There certainly can be no diffiulty with persons of ordi- "nary intelligence in drawing the distinction between sustain- " ing the Government itself, and sustaining or opposing those " who temporarily administer its affairs [i. e. the Adminis- " tration]. The latter is a question of party, the former of " patriotism."

Again, MR. SEWARD, Secretary of State, in his letter of November 10th, 1862, to MR. ADAMS, our Minister in England, says :

" It is a habit, not only entirely consistent with the Constitu- " tion, but even essential to its stability, to regard the Adminis- " tration, at any time existing, as distinct and separable from " the Government itself, and to canvass the proceedings of the " one without the thought of *disloyalty* to the other."

I have sometimes canvassed the proceedings of the Administration, but always *without one thought of disloyalty to the Constitution,* and MR. SEWARD expressly says this canvassing is "even essential to its stability." We find above that the Government is one thing and the Administration is quite another,—that our loyalty is entirely due to the Constitution, and it is our duty to maintain it in its integrity. From the commencement of the

Secession agitation, my only desire has been to see the question settled, so that UNION AND FRATERNITY would still exist! All my conversations and writings aimed at this one object. I have endeavored to be purely Patriotic. The Constitution knows no North and no South, and I have thought only of the benefits which will flow 'from A PRESERVED, *not a reconstructed Union.* Even if I had done a wrong, my offence must be slight, for I had never voted nor circulated tickets against the Administration : I had neither written for newspapers nor spoken at public meetings : my duties prevented my interfering in any way with elections, and yet my conduct is denounced by MR. STANTON as DISLOYAL, and it is extraordinary, that he will not allow me to see or get a copy of *the secret proceedings* upon which he charges me with DISLOYALTY—the Articles' of War to the contrary notwithstanding.

I speak of MR. STANTON, because I believe the PRESIDENT has too much business of more importance to engage his attention, than will permit him personally to investigate the allegations against Officers of the Army, except those high in rank, therefore, if he knows any thing whatever of my case he has obtained it through MR. STANTON, and of course, is the *ex parte* information, which MR. STANTON is unwilling to give me, as if ashamed of it.

The President, indeed, is authorized by act of Congress to dismiss officers, when in his opinion the good of the service may require it, but special orders No. 331 of July 25th 1863, says, I am dismissed for " disloyal conduct and the utterance of disloyal sentiments," and the evidence I have presented in this pamphlet will prove that this reason is incorrect and cannot be sustained. Then it is but right—it is a privilege clearly mine— to know exactly what this language means upon which I have been dismissed. And after I have assured MR. STANTON that I have not been DISLOYAL in conduct nor sentiments, and asked for an investigation—asked to be sent before the COMMISSION *which daily investigated the cases of dismissed officers, to ascertain whether the reports against them were false as the Accused had alleged*—it was my right—the Constitution guarantees a speedy trial ; the Articles of War provides for trial—it was a privilege of mine to have a hearing.

And I will venture to say that my dismissal rests upon the special' pleadings of Col. HOLT, the Judge Advocate General, whose implacable malignity, towards Gen. McCLELLAN, extends to those subordinate officers, who have a high regard for him. In my position, I had peculiar opportunities to observe the General's private character and worth, as well as military abilities. I have often made "grand rounds" of the Headquarters' Guards, at two o'clock in the morning and even later, and found the lights still burning in his tent, and the General engaged in his studies and duties of the field. I have seen and felt the enthusiasm which his presence among the soldiers has inspired, and heard their loud and heart-felt "huzzas!" I have frequently spoken of his merits, but even if he had lacked ability, I have thought the devotion to him, of the Army of the Potomac, was sufficient reason to retain him in the field, for it was worth thousands of soldiers. This, in the eyes of Col. HOLT, is no doubt a crime, and when the proceedings of his secret inquisition is dragged to light, and placed before the Public, it will be found that my greatest crime is, that I have been THE COMMANDANT OF GENERAL McCLELLAN'S HEADQUARTERS during his campaigns in Eastern Virginia and in Maryland.

I have presented the charges against me, and the testimony of many witnesses, and my services for nearly twenty four years, as overwhelming proof to rebut them. I now respectfully submit the case to the Public and ask them to judge between us. I have thought it but right to show that the trio, who have informed on me, prosecuted me, and condemned me, have by no means clean hands. And I respectfully, but most earnestly, protest against this mode of proceeding with the characters and honor of officers who have spent almost a quarter of a century in the U. S. Army.

www.ingramcontent.com/pod-product-compliance
Lightning Source LLC
Chambersburg PA
CBHW020310090426
42735CB00009B/1295